EVALUATING CHILDREN IN PRIMARY EDUCATION

NEERJA SHARMA
Reader,
Deptt. of Child Development,
Lady Irwin College
(University of Delhi)
Delhi - (India)

DISCOVERY PUBLISHING HOUSE
NEW DELHI - 110002 (INDIA)

First Published – 1997

Reprinted – 2023

ISBN: 978-81-7141-348-5

Evaluating Children in Primary Education

Published by:

DISCOVERY PUBLISHING HOUSE

4383/4B, Ansari Road, Darya Ganj

New Delhi-110 002 (India)

Phone: +91-11-23279245; 23253475; 43596065

+91 9811179893 / +91 9871656464

E-mail: discoverybooksindia@gmail.com

orderdphbooks@gmail.com

namitwasan9@gmail.com

web: www.discoverypublishinggroup.com

Printed at:

Infinity Imaging Systems

Delhi

CONTENTS

ACKNOWLEDGEMENTS

The close involvement of an experienced research team in questions of academic competence of children in the Government operated school system would, it was expected, became a catalyst for change in the right direction. This project was inspired by the zestful leadership given to educational and research endeavours by Mr. Anil Bordia, then Secretary of Education, Ministry of Human Resource Development, Govt. of India and supported with enthusiasm by Ms. Kiran Dhingra, then Director of Primary Education. To them a record of our appreciation, as well as to Mr. I.V. Subba Rao, Deputy Secretary and Mr. H.C. Baveja, Asstt. Educational Advisor in the Department of Education.

I wish to thank Dr. Satinder Bajaj, Director, Lady Irwin College for her wholehearted support for the project, from start to finish.

Among the officials who facilitated the operational aspects of the Project were Dr. L.P. Pandey, Director, Primary Education (U.P); Mr. Mahanand Mishra, Director, Upper Education, World Bank Project (U.P); Dr. B.K. Joshi, Director, Giri Institute of Development Studies, Lucknow; Dr. S.P. Jain, Director, NIPCCD, Lucknow; Director, Central Hindi Institute, Agra; and Basic Shiksha Adhikaris of Lucknow and Agra. I am grateful to them for their co-operation.

The Pilot Study was made possible with the co-operation from the Education Departments and schools of the NDMC, MCD, Delhi Administration and the U.P. Government, and of the Principals, teachers and children of Sardar Patel Vidyalaya and St. Xavier's School in Delhi and J.K.G. Happy School in Ghaziabad, U.P. I appreciate the help received from them.

I extend sincere thanks to Ms. Ranjana Goel, Ms. Kirti Jayaram and teachers of Sardar Patel Vidyalaya, Ramjas School, N.D.M.C. School (Babar Road) and MCD School (M.M.T.C. Colony) with whom useful discussions were held while preparing the tools for data collection.

When the study was being planned, it was with the clear understanding that Dr. Anandalakshmy, who was just handing over the Directorship of the Lady Irwin College and moving to Madras, would be the Chief Advisor, making herself available in Delhi at least once in two months for consultations with the team of research made up of myself as Faculty Coordinator and three Research Officers. Through several meetings, discussions, letters and occasional telephone calls – we kept the communications among us active and lively. We worked well as a team and learnt a great deal from each other.

The credit of sharing the processes of planning the study, field work and data analysis goes to the Research Officers. Ms. Mila Tuli and Ms. Vanya worked through the entire project period of 25 months, while Ms. Radha Pal and Ms. Dharini Lal worked for about half the period each. They were, in every sense, the pillars of the study and sincere appreciation of their role is recorded here.

Special thanks go to Dr. Nandita Chaudhary who was the consultant for the research design and analysis. Her interest in the project and her availability kept the morale of the team high. I am also grateful to Ms. Bhanumathi Sharma, Ms. Asha Singh, Dr. Kailash Khanna, Ms. Vinita Bhargava and Ms. Deepa Jain for their thoughtful contributions to this research.

Acknowledgements are due to Ms. Shraddha Shriniwas, Ms. Priti Joshi, Ms. Divya Lata and Mr. Vipul Tuli for coming to the rescue of the project team as field investigators at one point. Among the other field investigators who need special mention are Mr. Santosh, Mr. Anil, Ms. Indrani and Ms. Purnima.

I would like to thank Mr. K.S. Mehta and Ms. Rama Vani of International System Services who prepared the computer software according to our needs and undertook the analysis.

The credit of seeing through the quality and timely printing of the report goes to Mr. O.P. Sharma. I warmly acknowledge his support.

Thanks are also extended to Mr. Vijay Ram, Mr. Iqbal and Mr. Mahavir for their services at the office during the course of the project.

Neerja Sharma
Project Director,
Reader
Deptt. of Child Development,
Lady Irwin College
(University of Delhi)
New Delhi

LIST OF TABLES

LIST OF FIGURES

LIST OF APPENDICES

FOREWORD

The realization that primary education is **primary,** both in terms of State responsibility and of child development has, in recent years, set off ripples of concern. But until the ripples are converted into waves and the waves into energy, the concern will be nothing more than rhetoric.

The top heavy funding pattern in education with research institutions and selected Universities claiming a major part, ending in a feeble trickle to the Primary School System has received both exposure and critique.

While there are some signs that the Government will try to make amends for the sins of omission of earlier Plans – it becomes apparent that Primary Education has no powerful advocates to speak on its behalf. With the privatised section of the educational institutions catering to the demands of an articulate and upwardly mobile public, not to mention the traditional elite, the public sector Primary Schools suffer from neglect. The neglect is evident not merely from the low levels of funding. Even when funding is provided, the sanctions are missing. There is no accountability within the system – and the most powerless are the millions of children who look to the educational system with hope.

It is not that the under-privileged, dispossessed and poverty stricken child does not want an education. The greater tragedy is that he wants it and expects from it mobility, a vocation and a voice. It is this expectation that we squash a thousand times every day around the primary schools in the country.

The quality of the school environment, the training of the teachers, the nature and use of play equipment, the flexibility of the daily schedule, its responsiveness to the needs of children, the scope for the child's self-expression – the opportunities to develop a sense of self-esteem – myriad aspects constitute the components of a good educational system. In actuality, not even a modicum of this can be found in most schools. The heavy curriculum, the badly printed text books, the mechanical methods of teaching and testing – all these add to a school experience that makes dropping outlook like an act of courage and sanity.

Many programmes and prospects are now under progress to liven up the primary school, to provide the catalyst that may restore the school to a new equilibrium. This study was commissioned by the Department of Education, Ministry of Human Resource Development, with a suggestion that we try out different kinds of testing methods to identity if the basics have been acquired by the children of Class V. It was also to be a test of the Minimum Levels of Learning – the new launch of 1991 – that offered a standardised technique of assessing competencies.

A great deal of careful thought has gone into the execution of this study. It is offered to the discerning public with humility and hope.

Dr. S. Anandalakshmy
Consultant in
Child Development & Education

1

Introduction

The human child is one of the most remarkable outcomes of evolution. The exceptionality lies not only in that there is orderly development of organic matter from a minute cell to a complete human form, but also in that as every newborn grows, maturational changes unfold a fascinating array of abilities and skills.

The child grows in stages. Each stage seems perfect in itself. Yet it is only preparatory for what is coming next. Development is epigenetic : growth and differentiation of functions have nature's ground plan. Maturation follows a systematic and predetermined time table that is generally under the control of factors internal to the organism.

A child who is nurtured in a family develops naturally. Her parents and other members of the family foster her progress towards becoming an adult person. In childhood, she explores, learns, comprehends, changes and becomes increasingly aware of herself and her environment. She develops higher levels of intuition, insight, intelligence and affect according to Nature's agenda; caregivers can only support and nurture this grand scheme.

Of the several institutions that 'civilization' has introduced to the lives of children is formal education through the school system. Without delving into the history of ancient education or making a comparison with the purpose and quality of present day schools, it can be said that the socialization of the child without schooling is considered today as incomplete. A child who cannot or does not attend school at the 'right' age is seen as deprived or disadvantaged.

Education and Child Development

The prescription of school education for all children is made on the assumption that schools serve the goal of promoting the kind of learning that cannot be acquired without schooling. This belief was challenged by Illich (1971) who argued that schools were, in fact, hindering the child's development. He felt that "schools have alienated man from his learning"; the infrastructure and the system had become overwhelming and hence more important than the child. Illich wrote in favour of deinstitutionalizing education so as to free learning from school-systems, because "schools had made learning a specialized activity which it is not" (Illich, 1971). There is a feeling among some other thinkers also that the structure of education has taken precedence over the children who are to be educated.

However, the business of education cannot stop as nobody is convinced that the ritual aspects of schooling have overshadowed the learner's needs. It can be imagined that when schools came into being, its proponents were busy developing a curriculum and methods that would be appropriate for all children. Teaching became a profession, and it was sensible to have one teacher for a large group of children. The need to have training for teachers must have become apparent when the curiosity, creativity and imagination of a number of children could not be spontaneously handled by their teachers.

Education enables children realize their potential and to achieve the goal of self actualization. This humanistic goal gives precedence to the child over all means and methods in education. The buildings, school administrations, teachers and other personnel, syllabi and textbooks, furniture and uniforms exist because children need an education. This truism has been recognized in the Programme of Action of the National Policy on Education (1986), that states under its Implementation Strategies :

> ***"The country's faith in its future generations will be exemplified in the system of elementary education, which will get geared around the centrality of the child."*** **(p. 11).**

It is imperative, therefore, that early education must first allow the natural unfolding of the child's inherent talents and traits. Her own needs and interests should be the guiding principles of learning. Norms determined by a system unrelated to the child's own developmental stage and socio-cultural context can often suppress the child's quest for knowing.

The Goals of Primary Education

Primary education provides the fundamentals of all formal learning. The importance of the first few years of schooling has been recognized unequivocally in theories of Child Development and Education. Primary schools have a special responsibility for the intellectual and social development of our children. It is a responsibility shared with the family and community but the school is generally held accountable. Schools, therefore, need to ensure that children develop the competence and skills which will be the foundation of all their later education.

The importance of school in the life of a child cannot be underestimated. Schools should not just be a place where textbooks are read, tests are passed and skills acquired. It is a place in which a child makes friends, where games are played together and many interesting, even exciting things happen. It must be recognized that children are in school for a long time each day and for many months in the year and that the settings in which they are placed tend to be uniform. Not only is the classroom a relatively stable physical environment, it is also a fairly constant social context.

Despite the fact that thousands of children and adults are daily pressed into a student-teacher interface, we know very little about their interactions and the influence they have on each other. There is a great deal of literature available on educational practices, but we are still not aware of the wide range of happenings inside the classroom. What does a child feel when asked a question in class? What does she do when given a flexible assignment? Does the teacher make an effort to study the process of the child's answer or does she see it merely as 'right' or 'wrong'? What are the problems a child faces in learning?

An effective teaching-learning relationship requires as much intellectual intimacy as there is emotional intimacy in the parent-child relationship. Sensitivity and intimacy cannot be legislated into existence as we know too well. Curriculum can be defined but motivation cannot be promoted by command (Fromme, cited in Holt, 1990). And yet, that may be the key issue.

Learning in the Classroom

A variety of thinkers, writers and teachers like Ivan Illich, John Holt and Carl Rogers have often asked the question 'How much learning actually takes place in schools?' The answer to this question depends primarily on how learning is defined. Rogers in his book "Freedom to Learn" argues that learning is not "the lifeless, futile and quickly forgotten stuff that is crammed into the mind of a helpless child tied to his seat by bonds of conformity. It is, instead, the insatiable curiosity that drives a person to question and absorb everything he can see in his environment" (1983, p. 132). If this definition is accepted it has to be conceded that very little learning takes place in most schools.

Learning is a process. It is not only the act of seeing what the teacher is doing and then reproducing the same. Several cognitive processes including perception, association, recognition and recall are involved. Thus it is important that the material taught be presented so that a child can relate it to his own experiences. Careful observation of children in the classroom is necessary to find out what children really know and how they learn. Repeating mindlessly a set of words cannot be taken as knowledge of it. Real learning can be said to have taken place when a child is able to state the concept in her own words, see connections between it and other facts or ideas and solve a related problem. Citing an instance from a teacher's experience in a Mathematics class, Holt (1982) reported about a girl who was adept in doing simple addition of fractions from the textbook; but when asked by the teacher how many one-thirds constitute a whole, she replied, "it depends on how big the whole is".

One of the earliest 'lessons' a child learns in many a school is that it is shameful to give a wrong answer.. An answer must be 'right' whether the process is understood or not. Observations in the classroom reveal that when a child is called upon to solve a question, she does it quickly and fearfully, hands it to the teacher and awaits the verdict 'right' or 'wrong' ('not guilty' or 'guilty'). What hampers children's thinking and what drives them into narrow and defensive strategies is that they must please grown ups and teachers at all costs (Holt, 1982).

A field of knowledge, whether it be Maths, English or History is not just a matter of knowing all the items in the syllabus but of knowing how they relate to each other. As Rogers points out, "it is the difference between knowing the names of the streets in a city and being able to get from one place to another" (1983, p.132).

Besides enabling children to acquire knowledge and skill, a major responsibility of school is to provide an experience of schooling that is in itself enriching and satisfying. How far have schools in India been able to meet this responsibility ?

The Present Situation

Although universalization of primary education by the year 2000 is a clearly stated goal of the Government of India, the system is still characterized by inadequate facilities and insufficiencies in space, equipment, teaching etc. resulting in problems of children's absenteeism, failure and drop out. Conditions of economic deprivation in the family lead to hunger, malnutrition and ill-health of its members which, in turn, interfere with children's regular school attendance and with the ability to learn.

Another criticism of the educational planning is that it has not yet been adapted to the needs of society. Myron Weiner (1991) in a hard hitting critique of the Government's concern for children quotes a senior official as saying, *"We have an educational system that is not adequate for our society and a social system that obligates the poor people not to send their children to school." (p. 57).*

One of the explanations for our inadequate school system is that it has essentially been borrowed from the West and imposed on Indian conditions. As a result, school timings and examination schedules are not suited to the agricultural cycle, syllabi are inappropriate to what children see in the immediate environment and teaching is carried out in a language different from the languages and dialects spoken at home (Chitnis, 1987).

A look at recent educational surveys reveals the distressing status of primary education in India. Most schools are found in makeshift buildings with no drinking water or toilet facilities. Very often there are no teachers and sometimes only a single teacher who is usually overworked and underpaid (NCERT, 1986). In such conditions, what is indeed surprising is that children go to school at all, and not that one out of every two children drops out before Class V.

Another significant reason why the school system lacks effectiveness is because success of teaching is seen to depend upon how much of the curriculum a teacher can 'cover' in the course of the academic session. The more the facts from the textbook given to children, the higher the levei of teaching !

> *'Teach these boys and girls nothing but Facts. Facts alone are wanted in life. Plant nothing else and root out everything else'. The speaker, the schoolmaster and the third grown person present, all backed a little and swept with their eyes the rows of little vessels, then and there arranged in order, ready to have imperial gallons of facts poured into them until they were full to the brim."*
>
> Charles Dickens in *'Hard Times'*.

Rules and regulations too are considered ends in themselves rather than means to improving the quality of learning. It is due to these and other related factors that teaching in our primary schools is almost always dull and uninspired. Few questions are asked by the children and no discussion is allowed to take place. Punishment is frequent and humiliating.

Stress is laid on the formal educational qualifications of a teacher rather than on her personality traits. In primary school it is important that a teacher is sensitive to a child's need for free expression and spontaneity. In many cases, teachers are seen to have deeply ingrained prejudices regarding colour of skin, caste or socio-economic status. Societal prejudices are reinforced by them in the classroom. For example, poor performance is attributed to the child's lower class background.

Studies have shown how it is possible for the teacher to determine educability. The initial expectations of a teacher can determine the child's success or failure in school. Teachers possess a roughly constructed 'ideal type' necessary for a student to achieve 'success' in school. These characteristics are perceived by teachers as being related to the social class of a child (Entwisle, 1975).

Even though most teachers are aware that children have many responsibilities at home, these are ignored while giving 'homework'. The entire system is rigid and teachers too preoccupied with maintaining registers, doing paperwork and sorting out their own matters so that there is little time left for children (Chitnis, 1987).

As of now, the school-teacher system seems to be threatening and intimidating to the child; it often reduces an intelligent, alert and curious boy or girl to a school failure. All initiative is silenced. This further discourages the child and his family, who may not be keen on his attending school unwillingly at the "expense of his contributing to the family income".

Listlessness, boredom and apathy take the place of curiosity in the child. Interest, novelty and stimulating experiences lie outside the purview of the school. In order to foster learning in its true sense, it is essential that our educational system be made child centered and flexible.

Evaluation in Primary Education

Evaluation is an integral part of planning and implementing an educational programme. The purpose of evaluation is to make a judgement about the quality, reach and relevance of education. The aim is not simply to describe what students and teachers have done but is, instead, to gauge the level of achievement of a particular group of students, and to see how their performance compares with others. Evaluation has a diagnostic element which should highlight the strengths and weaknesses of the system. Most importantly, evaluation should provide feedback to teachers, students and planners. A good evaluation programme must also give guidance to teachers on modifications in teaching methods and materials.

Achievement tests are widely used in evaluating educational progress in the classroom. A test which has reliability and validity and is properly administered is a good indicator of a child's level of academic achievement. Since classroom test is the criterion measure, its structure and content are important.

Testing procedures and tools used in the country today leave a great deal to be desired. Firstly, there are very few standardized achievement tests in use and these are not freely available. Also, most of the tests which are in use are neither developmentally appropriate nor culturally suited to the needs of the range of subcultures of population for whom they are meant.

The content of tests is so entirely based on prescribed textbooks that even a slight deviation from the text results in dissonance and confusion in the minds of children and teachers alike. The format of a test and the 'type' of questions asked are the same year after year. What is essentially tested is how well a child is able to recollect his textbook material. The exact language used in the book is to be dutifully reproduced by the students. A 'creative' or 'novel' approach in answering a question may be marked wrong, since teachers are accustomed to scoring answers on the basis of how well they correspond with the textbook (Kamii, 1990).

How far the facts written in textbooks are relevant is also debatable. Textbooks and tests are based on nationally prescribed norms of learning.

The 'Levels of Learning' approach was introduced to provide to the educational system a set of guidelines for teaching children. By delineating the concepts to be taught to particular age groups of children, it aims to establish universal goals for teachers in the country. The concept of 'levels of learning' also promises to identify levels of achievement and thus introduce accountability in the system of instruction (NCERT, 1991). There has been a recent thrust in the Government's Policy to promote the application of Minimum Levels of Learning approach across the country. Several experimental projects are being supported by the Department of Education (Ministry of Human Resource Development) to implement competency-based teaching at the primary stage. The impact of these experiments is in the process of being assessed.

Testing Children

Achievement tests constructed for young children somehow seem to ask what a child does not know. A bright girl in the village may know all about the plants, trees and birds in her environment and about how a wheel helps to draw water from the well etc. However she is not asked about these things at all, but has instead to write a note about the importance of having a small family (MLL competency for Class III).

Questions are given one below the other in small print with no space for the child to work out her answer. There are no pictures or materials to engage children's interest. A child at the primary school level who developmentally has a short attention span may not even attempt to answer the dull and confusing questions.

A major drawback of most tests, especially achievement tests, is that it is difficult to infer competence directly from performance. Not only is the testing situation itself often alien and therefore an interference in performance, the items themselves may not be a good measure of the ability to be assessed. It is widely known that the contexts and situations in which competence is expressed are largely responsible for the differences in performances among different groups. However, few tests are sensitive to these issues.

Questions are generally stereotyped making it sufficient for a child to memorize a 'formula' answer. For example, by simply learning a rule in Maths a child may be able to subtract or multiply. But, ask him to calculate the year he was born from his present age he gets confused. This is because the concept underlying such mathematical operations is not clear to him. Examples given in class may also be far removed from the child's experience.

Lastly, the manner in which tests are administered, and the attitude of teachers and children toward tests needs emphasis. The word 'test' evokes fear and anxiety in children because they may fail. Tests are administered with such severity that a child develops a sense of fear and insecurity just at the mention of tests. Test results are seen by students as an end in itself and not as an opportunity to evaluate and find scope for improvement. The onus of these attitudes lies almost entirely with the school system. A class test is often administered as a form of punishment and children are labelled as 'bright' or 'dull' on the basis of results of one or two tests.

The goal of an evaluation programme should be to provide to every teacher a model within which students' performance can be assessed. Further teaching and planning of the institutional programme should be based on the assessment.

Once again in this education practice the child is important only as long as she is a part of a group of pupils who are subjects for evaluation. The individual child is a number and not a person. Thus it is said that **500** children were tested and not 500 **CHILDREN**. Above average and high achievers receive a different treatment compared to low achievers. For the former, the teacher would like to take credit, for the latter's performance, the child must take the blame.

The class test should be an important measure of evaluation, but it is rarely used to motivate students and to provide feedback to the teacher.

The Present Study

The present study was designed to develop a model for evaluating education at the primary level. The specific objectives of the study were:

1. To evolve a system of testing that is innovative and capable of replication.

2. To assess the levels of achievement of children in Class V in U.P. schools in Hindi, Arithmetic and Environmental Studies.

3. To identify the predictors of academic performance as related to school and teacher variables.

ON EDUCATION

"Literacy is not the end of education nor even the beginning. It is only one of the means whereby man and woman can be educated. I would therefore begin the child's education by teaching it a useful handicraft and enabling it to produce from the moment it begins its training. Thus every school can be made self-supporting, the condition being that the State takes over the creation of these schools."

Mahatma Gandhi

"In our childhood we imbibe our lessons with the aid of our whole body and mind, with all the senses fully active and eager. When we are sent to school, the doors of natural information are closed to us; our eyes see the letters, our ears see the abstract lessons, but our mind misses the perpetual stream of ideas which come from the heart of nature, because the teachers in their wisdom think that these bring distractions, that they have no great purpose behind them."

Rabindra Nath Tagore

2

The Schools and the Children

Population and Sample

The population under consideration in this study were children in Class V in government primary schools of Uttar Pradesh. These schools were run by the Basic Shiksha Parishad, in urban and rural areas. In 1986 there were 69,663 Primary schools under the purview of the Education Department in Uttar Pradesh (NCERT, 1986).

Within U.P., two districts were identified for the purpose of data collection. These were Lucknow and Agra. Detailed data on the educational characteristics of the two districts were collected. This was followed by discussions with State and District level officials dealing with primary education in U.P. On the basis of the information gathered, tentative decisions regarding the Blocks to be selected were taken. Certain prerequisites had to be taken care of in the selection of Blocks. These were as follows :

- Schools in both urban and rural areas must be covered.
- The rural Blocks must have an adequate number of government primary schools.
- The Blocks must be accessible by public transport.

Map of Uttar Pradesh

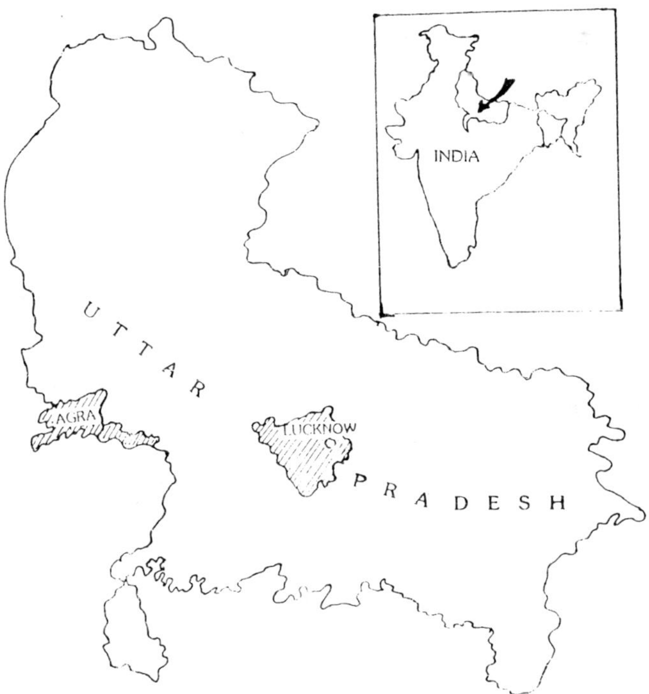

Map of District Lucknow

Map of District Agra

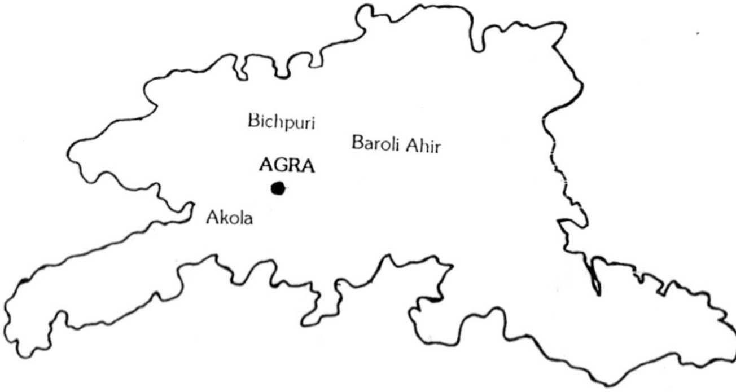

Sources: (i) Basic Shiksha Pragati Patrika (1990-91), Shiksha Vibhag, Agra.
(ii) Basic Shiksha Pragati (1990-91), Shiksha Nideshak, Lucknow.

These criteria were fixed to meet the major objectives of the study. The criterion of access was essential for researchability. To utilise the time available in the best way, rural Blocks with a large number of schools were preferred. Sample selection was thus governed by several ground realities.

The Blocks finally identified for field work are listed below :

District			*Block*
Lucknow	Urban area	:	Lucknow City
	Rural area	:	Chinhut Bakshi ka Talaab
Agra	Urban area	:	Agra city
	Rural area	:	Bichpuri Baroli Ahir Akola

Sample Selection : On the basis of lists of schools obtained from the District Education Offices of Lucknow and Agra, the sample schools were identified. Purposive sampling method was used to select the schools. The sampling criteria were as follows:

(i). A minimum of 15 children of Class V should be attending schools regularly.

(ii) Where two schools were located close to each other, i.e., within walking distance (making it possible to test children in two schools on the same day), the combined strength of children in Class V should not be less than 15.

(iii) The school should not be a private one.

Sample Size : The information from a reliable source in the Government based on enrolment figures was that, on an average, there would be 30 Class V children in U.P. government schools. Thus if 50 schools were covered in a district, it should have been possible to get a sample of approximately 1500 children per district. Sample size was to be determined by the number of children of Class V found in each school.

In 1991, there were 1046 schools (urban and rural) in Lucknow district run by the Basic Shiksha Parishad (BSP) with 26,819 children enrolled in Class V. In Agra, the number of schools run by the BSP was 1120 which had 36,949 children enrolled in class V*. Of these, a total of 2123 children, 998 from Lucknow and 1145 from Agra, constituted the sample. This sample was drawn from 47 schools in three blocks of Lucknow district and 57 schools in four blocks of Agra district (See Table 1a).

TABLE 1a

District-wise Distribution of Schools and Children in the Sample

District	*Number of Schools*	*Number of children*
Lucknow	47	998
Agra	57	1145
Total	104	2143

The following Table (1b) further shows the number of rural and u'ban schools in the two districts and the distribution of children in them.

TABLE 1b

Rural-Urban Distribution of Schools and Children of Class V in the Sample

	Rural	*Urban*
No. of Schools	54	50
No. of Children	1387	756
Mean no. of children in each school	25.7	15.1

* *Sources :*

(i) Basic Shiksha Pragati (1990-91) Lucknow mandal, Mandaliya Sahayak Shiksha Nideshak (Basic): Lucknow.

(ii) Basic Shiksha Pragati Patrika (1990-91), Shiksha Vibhag, Dvitiya Mandal, Agra.

As is evident, the average number of rural children attending class V at the time of testing (between January and April '92) was much higher (25.7) than the average number of urban children (15.1). As a result, in the total sample the proportion of rural children was almost twice that of urban children.

The total sample for the study comprised 2143 children. However, all 2143 children did not attempt all the three Achievement Tests. This is because the tests were administered on three different days to the children present in class V of the selected schools. The number of days that children were present varied from one to four. Even if a child attempted only one test (due to absence on other days) he or she was retained in the sample. As a result the total number of children taking the test in each subject was different. (See Table 2).

TABLE 2

Sample Size for the Achievement Tests

Achievement Test	*Number of Children*
Hindi	1980
EVS	1989
Arithmetic	1970

3

Construction of Achievement Tests

The primary aim of this project was to develop an evaluation model that is creative, culturally relevant and grade-specific, but not textbook-dependent. This entailed the preparation of Achievement Tests in Hindi, Environmental Studies (EVS) and Arithmetic (Appendix III).

Achievement Tests : Class V is the last stage in primary school. In order to comment on the educational status of children at the end of Class V, it was decided to test them for competencies expected at the end of Class IV and the beginning of Class V.

The Achievement Tests were developed through a rigorous process that involved the following steps :

- A review of the curriculum, textbooks and other material for Classes IV and V.
- The construction of an item pool.
- Holding workshops and individual meetings with school teachers from both government and private schools, with experts in the field of Child Development and other resource persons to evaluate the items.
- Preparation of a draft of the tests by incorporating the suggestions provided.
- Preliminary trial with a few children (pre-pilot study) and

subsequent preparation of a revised version of the test.

- A pilot study on 479 children in Delhi and Ghaziabad (U.P.), to assess item validity.

- Development of a computer programme for statistical analysis.

Four drafts of the tests were prepared, each one an improved version over the previous one, before the Achievement Tests were finalized for field testing. This process was completed over four months. (See Appendix IX : Pilot Study Report).

The following guidelines were used while developing the Achievement Tests :

- Developmental norms for 9-10 year old children.
- Syllabi and textbooks for Classes IV and V.
- Minimum Levels of Learning at Primary Stage (NCERT, 1991).

Using these guidelines, the areas of learning to be assessed were identified. An item pool was developed in each area for the three subjects Hindi, EVS and Arithmetic.

In order to optimise children's performance it was necessary to ensure that the testing procedure, including the test booklets, would not be perceived as an examination. It was considered important to use a method of assessment that did not appear like the conventional examination procedure. The booklets and administration methodology were to be child-friendly and non-threatening.

No existing tool for children in class V was found to satisfy this condition. It was therefore decided to develop test instruments using the following criteria :

Each item was grade-specific and age-specific (prerequisite for criterion referenced testing), ***rather than text book-dependent***. Competencies in the areas of learning specified according to the three criteria mentioned earlier, were assessed through items that were interesting compared to the standard textbook items. The purpose was to make every child feel challenged and to hold his/her interest. The child should want to attempt the booklet and not put it away because it is too difficult or too simple. A wide range of items had to be included to meet this objective. Interest was also sustained by presenting the items in the form of stories and puzzles along with pictures and illustrations.

As far as possible, the items included in the booklets were related to the child's daily life - a part of the socio-cultural context within which the child grows and develops.

Creativity was another important component of the procedure adopted for item development. While it is based on sound educational principles that a creative and interesting way of doing anything would increase the motivation and optimise the performance of children, the incidental learning that also takes place during such situations is not always recognized. Children are active learners; they pick up bits and pieces of information from every situation – even from Achievement Tests!

In the process of item development, ***care was taken to see that no form of bias (socio-cultural or gender) was reflected in any of the items***. The procedure for test administration was also carefully planned. This has been described in a later section.

An important step in the development of the testing procedure was that a Practice Booklet was prepared. Each child answered it on the day of rapport formation as a form of practice. The booklet had a few items in all three subjects and the children were helped if they had difficulty while answering any questions (Appendix II).

Scoring : Scoring booklets for all three subjects (Language, EVS and Arithmetic) were prepared indicating the scoring patterns and listing all possible responses for each item (Appendix IV a, b & c).

Each test item had a three-point scoring system, i.e. 0, 1 or 2. A score of 0 was given for an incorrect response, no response or an unclear response. A score of 2 was given if there was a correct or acceptable response. A partially correct response was given a score of 1. No negative marking was done.

For items that had many sub-parts, (i.e. Q. 5 in the Language booklet) the total number of possible correct responses for these sub-parts were grouped to fit into the three scores. In the above example, there are five sub-parts. The scoring was done as follows :

No. of correct responses	*Score*
None or 1	0
2 or 3	1
4 or 5	2

The maximum possible score in each of the three subjects (Hindi, EVS and Arithmetic) was 50.

Interview Schedule for Teachers : In addition to the Achievement Tests, an interview schedule was prepared to obtain information from teachers regarding the size of the school, its infrastructure and other facilities available, the teachers' training status, the nature of instructional methods used and their preparation for teaching (Appendix V a & b). It was expected that these facts about the school and the teachers would be important correlates of children's achievement levels.

Pilot Study

A pilot study was conducted by the core team between August and October 1991 with the objective of establishing the validity of the Achievement Tests and the testing procedure. This study was carried out on children of Class V in government and private schools at Delhi and Ghaziabad (U.P). On the basis of the results obtained, certain modifications were made in the test format and procedure before the testing programme for the study in U.P. was finalized (Pilot Study Report).

4

Testing Children in Primary Schools

Data Collection : Data collection for the final study in U.P. was carried out between January 20, 1992 and April 28, 1992. Fieldwork in Lucknow district took 40 days while a total of 55 days were spent in district Agra (inclusive of all holidays).

A team of three Research Officers and nine Field Investigators undertook field work. The Field Investigators were selected and trained in Lucknow for data collection and they worked in both districts.

Training of Personnel : A two-day training workshop was conducted by the core staff for the field investigators. During the workshop they were familiarized with the project, the Achievement Tests and the testing procedure. Practical training continued in the field for the first week of data collection. The entire project team was divided into three groups. Each group had three Field Investigators and one Research Officer. The Research Officers demonstrated the testing procedure within the classroom. Subsequently, when it was felt that the Field Investigators were fairly conversant with the procedure, the group was divided into four teams (of three members each). Each team was to take up a school for data collection and work there for four days before moving on to the next school.

Testing Methodology : The testing team for each school consisted of two or three persons. The team spent four days in each school since the testing programme comprised of four sessions with the students.

Development of a method with a difference was one of the focal points in this research project. The guiding factor in preparing the tools for testing and in administering these was to bring out optimal performance in children despite the constraint of their unfamiliarity with the procedures and the persons. Unfamiliar people and situations may increase the anxiety of young children and thus influence their performance on any task.

As the first step towards keeping test anxiety to a minimum, the Achievement Tests were not introduced as 'tests' to the school authorities and the students. They were told that the research team had prepared some puzzles for children. These puzzles were based on three subjects – Hindi, EVS and Arithmetic, and were put together in three different booklets titled : बूझो तो जानें 1, 2 and 3.

The administration strategy was such that it did not appear to be a 'test' to children.

- *One full school day was spent in establishing rapport with children.*
- *Only one test was administered on each day. This was done to avoid fatigue, which could have an effect on children's performance on the second and third tests.*
- *There was no time limit for completing the tests. Children were allowed to work at their own pace. The time taken by each child was recorded on the child's test booklet. The researchers were not coercive or threatening in any way. They were friendly and willing to answer queries of children on taking the test, but they did not help by giving the answers. They did not simply distribute the test booklets and then sit in one place. They moved around the class among the children and observed them as they were writing. In general they communicated friendliness in their demeanour.*

A Testing Module : On the first day of data collection the testing team carried a weighing scale and a measuring tape to the school. ***Measuring Class V children's height and weight was used as the introductory activity.*** The researchers first initiated a discussion with children by asking them if they knew their own weight or height, how these measurements were taken, and if they had seen the measuring instruments. This was followed by discussing whether height or weight increases or decreases and how this happens. The kind of scales people usually come across at railway stations, cinema halls, hospitals etc. were also discussed. The weighing scale brought by the team was shown to the children and the method of measuring and reading the measurement from the scale was demonstrated to them.

The actual task of taking weights and heights was undertaken by the children. They came in pairs and took each other's measurements. The researchers assisted them in taking the readings. This reading was recorded in a register by one of the researchers. Children could verify their weight or height with this record if they forgot their measurement. On an average in a class of 15-20 children, this activity took 45 minutes to one hour. By the time this exercise was over the children and researchers became quite comfortable with one another. A rapport was thus formed.

Following this, the children were given an orientation to familiarize them with the format of the test. Some items prepared for this session were solved on the blackboard with the children participating in the exercise (Appendix I). They were encouraged to ask questions and to clarify their doubts. Subsequently a Practice Booklet, containing items similar to these, was given to each child to work on. It was an exercise to be scored, though the scores were not to be used for formal analysis.

Guidelines for using the Practice Booklet were given before the children started attempting the questions therein. Every child was given a number (on the basis of the order they were sitting in) to be written on the cover page of their booklet. This number alongwith the child's name was also noted in a register carried by the researchers. The children were asked to remember the number given to them since they would use it for the other booklets also.

The first page of the booklet, which sought information such as the child's name, age, gender, school etc. was filled simultaneously by all the children with guidance from the researchers. Once this was done and the children had started answering the questions, the researchers would go around the classroom checking if the children had any problems and answering their queries.

After the children had completed their work, the researchers spent some time talking with them. They sought children's reactions to the activities carried out with them and reminded them that they had to attend the remaining three days' sessions. ***They were also told that children who attended all three sessions would receive a pencil on the last day.*** Eventually every child present on the last day received a pencil.

On the second day the Achievement Test in Hindi was given to the students. It had been planned to administer the Hindi Test before the others because this test was developed with illustrations of comic strips and pictures which can hold children's attention. It was felt that this would motivate children to attend the other two sessions as well.

Item 13 of the Hindi Test was an individual oral item. For this item one researcher spent some time with each child. In this, the child had to make up a small story or describe what was happening in the picture shown. Since the item was an oral one, the child's responses were recorded on an audio cassette. Of the testing team of three members, two remained in the classroom and administered the group test, while one member carried out the oral test in a relatively quiet place away from the classroom.

On completing the test the children would bring their booklets to the researchers. The researchers went through each child's booklet and ascertained that he or she had answered it fully. In case it was found that the child had not attempted a particular question or a set of questions, the child was encouraged to go through it again and try to answer.

Children who completed their work well before the others were asked to make any drawing on a blank page at the end of the test booklet. This ensured that they would not disturb the other children who were still working.

The EVS Test was given to children on the third day in the school. On the fourth day, the Arithmetic Test was administered. When all the children completed this booklet, a pencil was given to each one of them as a token of appreciation. During the four days spent at each school, the class teacher was interviewed about her/his teaching schedule, daily routine and the facilities available in the school.

The Achievement Test booklets were not scored at the school, but after returning from data collection. Scoring was done invariably on the same day using the scoring key. The oral testing responses were transcribed from the audio cassettes and then scored by the researchers.

When data collection in a particular school was over, the answer booklets were compiled. The three test booklets of each child were put together and made into sets on the basis of predetermined serial numbers and code numbers developed for data analysis.

Method of Analysis

Descriptive and statistical analyses were undertaken to analyse the data collected. Descriptive analysis was used for the school and teacher data and inferential analysis was done with the scores of children on the Achievement Tests.

Software was especially designed to organise the data for computerised analysis. Before data entry in the computer, all the data sheets, i.e. students' score sheets in the three subjects, teachers' response sheets and school data sheets, were coded. This information was then entered using the format and a programme developed for the project.

The students' performance on Achievement Tests was analysed in the following dimensions :

- Overall performance of children on the three tests.
- Levels of performance on each item and each area of learning in the three tests.
- Rural - urban differences
- Gender differences

The 't' test was used to determine the significance of difference in students' performance with reference to the variables under study.

The teacher and school data were examined to identify factors that could be seen as correlates of children's performance.

5

Findings : The State of Schools

A Profile of Schools

The experiences and encounters of the research team during the period of data collection were varied – each reflecting the ethos of the institution or region; while also giving an insight into the problems affecting primary education in India.

The following section describes the features of the schools visited that we believe have a bearing on children's education.

Enrolment vs Attendance : A list of schools being run by the Shiksha Parishad was provided by the District Education Officers in Lucknow and Agra. This list provided information about the number of schools in each Block and the number of children in each school. This number was actually the enrolment figure. From our experience of school visits, the actual attendance figure of children in Class V may be placed between 40-50% of the enrolment figure, or even less in some schools.

During school visits also, teachers tended to equate enrolment figures with attendance figures. When teachers were asked about the number of children in Class V, the register was produced to show the figure. However, further probing would reveal a different picture of partial attendance.

There were many instances of the school authorities portraying a false image of the strength of Class V in the school. In the districts of

The Agra Episode – Managing Within the System

In Agra, there were several instances where school authorities brought in some private school children to show a higher attendance in Class V. These children had been coached to say that they studied in that government school.

The research team also came across Government schools which seemed to be functioning not so much to impart education but to provide security to some 'teaching shops'. Children were enrolled in the government school but they studied in a nearby private school. On a visit to a particular school in Agra, very few children were found present in Class V. The authorities at this school said that a number of children were absent that day and if the researchers began work on the following day, they would find many more children. This would be done by contacting the children personally and asking them to attend school for the next four days.

On the following day, when the team entered the classroom, children sitting in the front row said "Namaste" but most of the other children said "Good morning madam". A couple of children were in a school uniform. Sensing that something was unusual, the researchers asked the children which school they attended regularly. All of them named the government school, but looked uneasy. When asked to name some of their classmates, they were unable to name those sitting in the front row and did not seem comfortable with them.

While working with these children it was possible to observe differences between the two groups within the class quite distinctly. Some children were more articulate than the others and also used some English terms. Later, it was learnt from one of the children that he attended a school called 'Vidya Mandir' close to the government school and had been sent here along with other children by his teachers. One child, who was a regular student of the government school, said that there were only four children in her class and all the other children had been called from somewhere else.

The school teachers still insisted that all the children were students of the governmemt school. One of them said that the children went to the private school only 'for tuition'. He opened the school register and read out the names of the children. According to him, the parents had their children's names registered in the government school. But it was upto the parents to decide where to send their children.

This episode revealed a well organized collaboration between the government and private schools. Children were enrolled in the government school on the advice of the private school authorities, but they studied in the private school and paid fees to the private school only. Since the private school was not recognised, a way had been found to recognize the schooling given by this school. The 'adjustment' was profitable for both the groups involved. Enrolling children in the government school ensured them a chance to take class V board exams and obtain a certificate recognized by the education system in the state. The teachers in the government school could show on record that their school was functioning very well since there were 35-40 children on the records of class V even though there were only four children studying in class V of the governmeht school.

Lucknow and Agra, at times teachers would send some children from Class IV to Class V. If this was discovered during or after testing, it was suggested that they could be dropped from the sample.

School Timings – A matter of teachers' convenience : One feature repeatedly observed during data collection was the irregular school timings in a majority of the schools visited. This was especially true of schools in the rural areas. Schools would open and close at the whim of the teachers. Very often, schools were found closed at 10.30 - 11.00 a.m. although officially they were supposed to follow the summer schedule of working from 7.00 a.m to 12.00 noon.

While teachers in the rural schools attributed this to the long distances they had to travel from the city to reach the school, the same excuse could not be given for urban schools. Besides attending to personal work, teachers would leave early or close the school when they were required to attend meetings with the BSA (Basic Shiksha Adhikari), their Cluster Heads or other officials in the Blocks.

Once the researchers walked for about 3 kms. to a school in Takhwa (Lucknow) to find the school closed at 10.30 a.m because the teachers had to go to a meeting in another village. There were many other instances when the research schedules were disrupted because of unscheduled closure of schools.

School Schedules – Vacation and working days : A major problem faced by rural schools was that the school timings were not suited to the agricultural cycle of this area.

In the month of April, during data collection in Agra, school attendance was found to be very poor. In the harvesting season, the children were busy working in the fields as harvesting generally requires a collective effort from the entire family.

Infrastructure of the School

Whenever there is a discussion on the state of primary schools in India, emphasis is given to the sorry state of schools in the rural parts of the country.

The experience during data collection in the two districts of U.P. showed that the condition in urban areas was worse than that in rural schools contrary to general expectations. A large number of school buildings in the city were unsafe, but classes continued to function there. Surprisingly, this was also the state of a particular school at walking distance from the Basic Shiksha Adhikari's Office in Agra.

In a school in Lucknow classes had to be suspended during the monsoons as the ceiling leaked. Repair work had not been carried out because, according to the reason given by the Headmaster, the department did not have sufficient funds. There was a distinct difference between schools in the two areas in terms of the space provided for the school. In the city schools, classrooms were small and insufficient in number. More than one class had to be conducted in one room or in a corridor and taught by different teachers. Only a few schools had open space outside for the children to play since many of them were located in narrow, crowded residential localities. The noise level from the surroundings was always high in these schools. This was in sharp contrast to the commonly encountered surroundings in the rural areas.

In the rural schools, even if there were insufficient number of rooms, there was at least plenty of open space available. Classes would be held in the shade of trees. Children could play in the large open grounds surrounding the school buildings, which was rarely possible in the urban areas.

Another difference was that in rural schools drinking water was freely available to children either in the schools or just outside the school premises. This minimal facility was lacking in a number of urban schools.

The facilities required for teaching children were inadequate in both urban and rural schools. In many schools there was no blackboard. If a blackboard was there chalk would be rarely available.

Floor mats for the children to sit on were insufficient. The team came across several instances where the teachers had collected money and bought mats for the school. This was done after repeated requests to the Education Officers had failed to evoke positive response. In a school in Lucknow, school furniture was made and even a room was constructed from funds collected by the community.

Teaching aids, even when they were available, were not used with the children. In the primary school at Tora (Agra), blocks, puzzles, teaching aids for science were lying untouched in locked cupboards. They were not used for fear of 'spoiling' or losing them.

Problems of Teachers

During the period of data collection, the team visited 104 schools and met and spoke to the teachers working in these schools. Talking to them helped in understanding the functioning of their schools and the teachers' problems and expectations. It also helped in identifying the factors that contributed to the unfortunate state of affairs in school after school.

It cannot be said that all the teachers were unenthusiastic. Many of them were actively interested in their work. Some of them tried to make the best of what they had, but most of them had also resigned themselves to the reality of the situation. The teachers were articulate about their problems and a few even gave these to us in writing so that we should pass them on to the higher authorities at the district level. Most schools had fewer teachers employed than the number sanctioned. As a result one teacher would take many classes simultaneously, i.e. the children from different classes sitting together and being taught by one teacher.

Whenever the teachers were indifferent and uninterested, and had irregular attendance and timings, the children suffered. Attendance of children would be low, their reactions to schooling denoted boredom and apathy. Clearly the behaviour of the teachers was reflected in the attitudes and reactions of the children to school (see box).

Private Tuitions for Attention in the Classroom

The attitudes of the teachers towards their work and students can be assessed from the following incident. In a school in Agra, we were told that if a child not taking tuition from the class teacher raised a query, the teacher would scold and /or hit the child. The teacher would call the parents of such a child and tell them that the child was weak in studies and required coaching. The parents were left with no other alternative but to send the child for tuition to this teacher. Following this , the teacher would pay attention to the child in class, praising him/her for being bright.

A high incidence of corporal punishment was observed in the schools. Slapping children across the face or beating them on their bodies was a common part of the disciplining. According to the teachers, physical punishment was the only method to discipline "these children". "इन पे तो डंडे का ही असर होता है।" "लातो के भूत बातों से नहीं मानते" * was heard time and again.

Children's Reactions to the Research Team

Contrary to the usual response of anxiety and apprehension in a testing situation, children in all schools had a positive response to the researchers and their work. At the end of each session they would ask when the team would visit their school again.

Everyday, at the end of the testing session, a number of children would follow the team to the school gate or boundary and at times even outside the school. On successive days, the number of children coming to school would increase. Children of Class V would inform their other classmates, who had been absent, about the work being done. This created an interest in them to come to the school the next day too.

In many schools, the children became very friendly with the researchers and would talk to them freely. During such conversations they expressed their resentment towards the teachers. They viewed their teachers as punitive and harsh, who did not help them to understand what was taught. Some children even asked the researchers to become their teachers because they were patient with them – "आप तो मारते भी नहीं हो, प्यार से समझाते हो"**

Performance on Achievement Tests

The tests were scored and coded according to the guidelines discussed earlier. Table-3 gives the scores of children's performance on the Hindi, EVS and Arithmetic Achievement Tests.

---

* Nothing works with these children except a beating.

** You don't even hit us, you explain things gently.

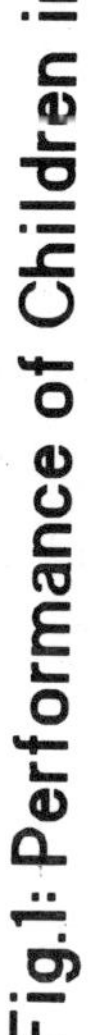

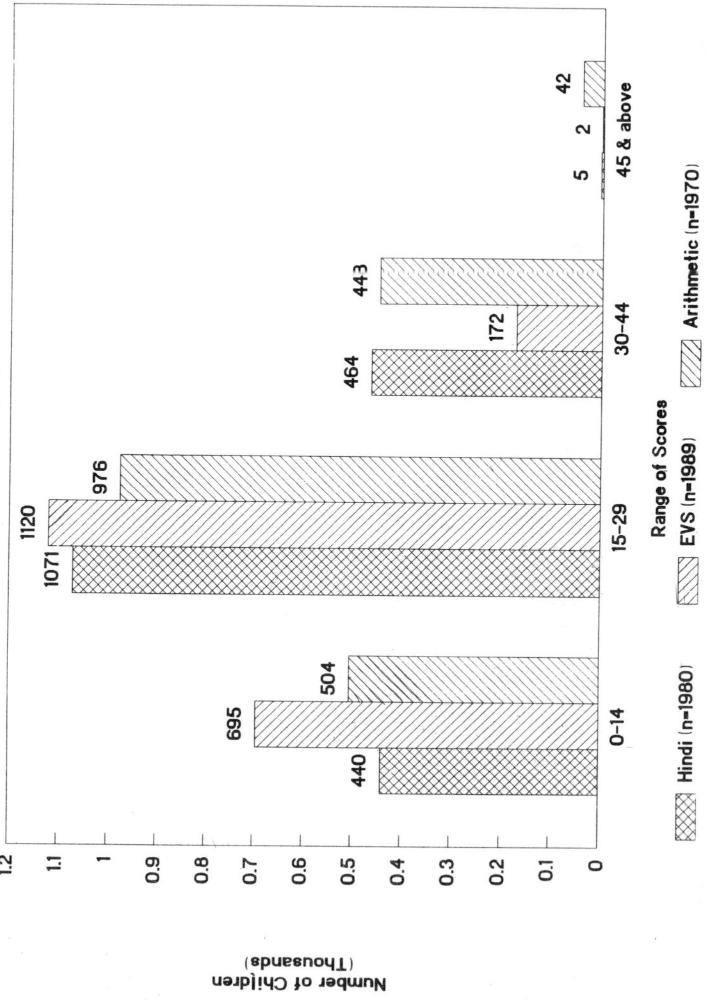

Fig.1: Performance of Children in
Hindi,EVS and Arithmetic

TABLE 3

Overall Performance in Hindi, EVS and Arithmetic

	Hindi	*EVS*	*Arithmetic*
Number of Students	1980	1989	1970
Mean Score	22.25	18.13	22.10
Standard Deviation	9.25	8.03	10.51
Paired t values :	[Hindi-EVS]	[EVS-Arithmetic]	[Hindi-Arithmetic)
't' calculated	23.62*	-20.7*	-0.77
't' critical = 2.575			

* Significant at $\alpha = 0.01$
Maximum marks = 50

It is apparent that the over all performance of children was low; below 50% in all areas. Their performance was higher on the Hindi and Arithmetic tests compared to EVS. The difference in performance between Hindi and Arithmetic was not significant.

Low scores in EVS mean that children found this Achievement Test difficult even though it consisted of items pertaining to their immediate physical and social environment. This indicates that either no attention is paid to this subject or that the teaching of EVS is unsatisfactory. What is taught in the classroom is unrelated to the natural environment of the child. A meaningful connection between EVS and the environment is not demonstrated by the teacher in the classroom. The emphasis seems to be on memorising specific 'answers' from the textbook and reproducing the same when tested. Information from the text is not communicated by the teacher. Only a few children had text books and these were rarely used. It seems that the teachers did not pay the same attention to teaching EVS as to Language and Arithmetic.

Levels of Performance

Performance in the 80% or above range is taken to be mastery of a subject (NCERT, 1991). An analysis of scores of children reveals

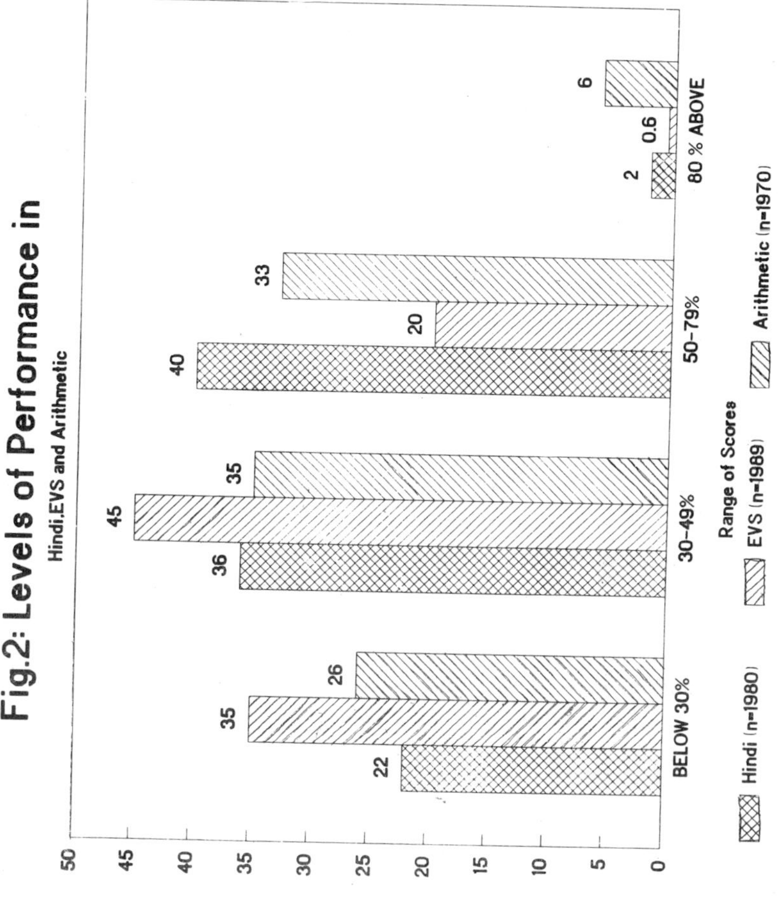
Fig.2: Levels of Performance in
Hindi,EVS and Arithmetic
Percentage of Children
50
45
40
35
30
25
20
15
10
5
0
22
35
26
36
45
35
40
20
33
2
0.6
6
BELOW 30%
30-49%
50-79%
80 % ABOVE
Range of Scores
Hindi (n=1980)
EVS (n=1989)
Arithmetic (n=1970)

that a very small percentage of the total sample have attained the mastery level (See Table - 4). In order to ascertain the achievement profile of the children, their performance has been graded at three lower levels as well.

TABLE 4

Levels of Performance in Hindi, EVS and Arithmetic

Subject	*Number of children scoring*			
Percentage	Below 30%	30%-49%	50%-79%	80% and above
(Score)	(Below 14)	(15 – 24)	(25 –39)	(40 –50)
Hindi (n = 1980)	440 (22.2%)	716 (36.2%)	782 (39.5%)	42 (2.1%)
EVS (n = 1989)	695 (34.9%)	886 (44.5%)	397 (20%)	11 (0.6%)
Arithmetic (n = 1970)	504 (25.6%)	695 (35.3%)	656 (33.3%)	115 (5.8%)

Note : The maximum score being 50 for each test, each point on the scale represents a value of 2 per cent.

Performance below 29% : This category includes scores below 15 out of a maximum of 50 marks. In Hindi, the percentage of children performing at this level was 22.2% whereas in EVS and Arithmetic it was 34.9% and 25.6% respectively (Table 4). By implication approximately one fourth of the children studied could not even obtain 30% on the tests. The 30% level can be considered the same as the 'pass-percentage' for formal examinations.

Performance between 30% and 49% levels : This category included any score between 15 and 24 out of a maximum of 50 marks. In the three Achievement Tests, the percentage of children achieving between 30 and 49 per cent levels was 36.2% in Hindi, 44.5% in EVS and 35.3% in Arithmetic. It is evident that this category includes the largest number of children.

Performance between 50% and 79% : Performance at this level indicates a score between 25 and 39 out of a maximum score of 50.

Examining the scores of children, Table 4 shows that 39.5% of the children fall in this category in Hindi, 20% in EVS and 33.3% in Arithmetic. This implies that more than half the total number of children who attempted the achievement tests had a performance level below 50%.

Performance at the 80% level & above : Of the 1980 children who attempted the Hindi test, only 2.1% (42 out of 1980) were able to score more than 80% (i.e. a score of 40 or more out of a maximum score of 50). In EVS, a mere 0.6% (11 out of 1989) of the children appeared to have mastered the competencies. Only 5.8% children (115 out of 1970) scored about 80% in Arithmetic.

Area-wise Performance

The term 'area' as used in the following discussion implies a group of related items which constitute a particular topic within Hindi, EVS and Arithmetic.

The performance of children has been analysed in terms of weighted mean score for each item or group of items (area). **Weighted mean** refers to the ratio between the actual score obtained by children and the maximum score that can be achieved, expressed as a percentage. It is the level of children's performance on an item or a set of items.

Performance in Hindi : Table 5a depicts the performance of children in six major areas into which the test items in Hindi have been classified. In this Achievement test, the items pertaining to Grammar elicited the highest percentage performance i.e. 62.2%. A total of 75.2% children were able to score at this level.

TABLE 5a

Area–wise Performance in Hindi

Area	*Listening (Comprehension & Memory)*	*Speaking*	*Writing*	*Comprehension of of ideas through reading*	*Grammar*
Item No.	1, 2, 3.1, 3.2, 3.3	13	4,12	9.1, 9.2, 9.3 9.4, 9.5, 10, 11	5, 6, 7, 8
Weighted mean (%)	61	28	22.3	47.5	62.2

Writing synonyms and antonyms (item 5 and 6), correcting grammatical errors in given sentences (item 7), matching masculine words with appropriate feminine ones (item 8), were the items constituting this area. In doing an item analysis it was found that the highest performance (70.2%) was obtained on item 8, but on item 7, the performance was the lowest within this competency (57.7%). It was clear that children's performance on items requiring application of the rules of functional grammar (correcting grammatical errors) was much lower than that on other items in this area.

The performance was lowest on the area of writing (22.3%) indicating that this skill was the least developed. Weighted mean of 13.9% reflects that writing a guided composition was difficult. It is significant to note that where children were expected to describe a given picture orally, the performance was at the level of 28.1%.

The weighted mean in the area of comprehension was about 47%. Where the items required comprehension of ideas from a written passage and also from stories represented graphically through comic strips, the performance ranged from 25.1% to 71.1%. Wherever the answer could not be picked up directly from the passage and required the children to use their reasoning or imagination (item 9.5) the performance was low (25.4%) (refer to Table 5b in Appendix VI for more detail.)

The results indicate that children attending these schools are at a loss when they have to attempt problems requiring divergent thinking, originality and spontaneity. It appeared that opportunities for and experiences in free expression were not provided to them as part of their education. It was disheartening to see that that children who appeared to be perfectly fluent in language usage would submit their booklets without answering the items that required original writing.

Performance in EVS : The performance of children on the EVS test is shown in Table 6a. Among the items tested, map-reading got the lowest score i.e. 10.3%. Although maps have received emphasis in textbooks and syllabi of classes IV and V, item 14.2 (identification of two states on the map of India with the help of cues) elicited an extremely low performance of 3.8%.

TABLE 6a

Area–wise Performance in EVS

Area	*Means of Transport*	*Energy*	*Plant Life*	*Animal Life*	*Communication*	*Calendar*	*The Universe*	*Map Skills*	*Geography*	*Properties of Matter*
Item Nos.	1, 2	3	4.1 4.2 4.3 17.2	5, 6	7.1, 7.2 8, 17.1	12	13	14.1, 14.2, 14.3	14.4, 16	9, 10, 11, 15
Weighted mean(%)	66.0	12.9	32.3	45.8	36.8	52.6	37.7	10.3	38.3	38.9

On the items related to types of energy, uses of plants, states and cities, the weighted mean was less than 20%.

The scores were highest on items which involved recall from day-to-day observations such as classifying means of transport or animals into given categories (Table 6b in Appendix VI).

Performance in Arithmetic : In the Arithmetic test, children performed relatively well on items that required knowledge of one or two of the basic operations such as addition, subtraction, multiplication and division (Table 7a). However, the area that required the application of these operations – the items on daily life problems, received low scores. Fractions were the most difficult for the children as can be seen in the low performance in this area 36.3% (for details see Table 7b in Appendix VI).

Performance as Assessed Against MLL Competencies

As has been mentioned earlier, the competencies tested in different subjects included some given in the Minimum Levels of Learning document (NCERT, 1991). Tables 8a, b & c illustrate the items in the three subjects that correspond to the MLL items. Mastery level in a subject in the MLL document is defined as 80% children obtaining a score of 80% or more. This was not attained in any competency in any of the subjects in the present study.

TABLE 7a

Area–wise Performance in Arithmetic

Areas	*Number Concept*	*Addition, Subtraction, Division, Multiplication*	*Daily Life Problems*	*Fractions*
Item Nos.	2.1, 2.2 2.3, 2.4 3, 4	5, 6, 7.1, 7.2	8.1, 8.2, 9, 10, 11, 12, 13.1, 13.2, 14.1, 14.2	15, 16.1, 16.2, 17
Weighted Mean (%)	43.7	64.6	39.7	36.3

TABLE 8a

Performance of Children on Hindi Items Corresponding with MLL Competencies

Item No.	*Area*	*Corresponding MLL Competency*	*% of children performing*	*Weighted Mean (%)*
1.	Listening	1.4.3	72.6	49.9
2, 3.3	Listening (Comprehension & Memory)	5.4.1	67.7	58.7
3.2	Listening (Comprehension & Memory)	5.4.2	74.3	74.3
4	Writing	4.4.2	71.7	56
12	Writing	4.4.3	40.9	13.9
9.1, 9.2	Comprehension	5.4.1	50	46.1
9.3, 9.4	of ideas	5.4.2		
9.5	through reading			
10, 11	Reading	3.4.1	53.1	50.75
13	Speaking	2.4.1 2.4.3	94.8	28

TABLE 8b

Performance of Children on EVS Items Corresponding with MLL Competencies

Item No.	*Area*	*Corresponding MLL Competency*	*% of children performing*	*Weighted Mean (%)*
3	Energy	9.5.1	19.1	12.9
4.2	Plant Life	8.4.1	20.9	13.9
4.3	Plant Life	8.3.4	78.3	58.8
6.	Animal Life	8.3	86.9	60.9
10.	Properties of matter	9.4	69.9	47.7
9.	Properties of matter	9.4.2	67.6	33
11	Properties of matter	9.4.3	51.7	43.3
14.4, 16	Geography	4.4.1	48.9	38.4

TABLE 8c

Performance of Children on Arithmetic Items Corresponding with MLL Competencies

Item No.	*Area*	*Corresponding MLL Competency*	*% of children performing*	*Weighted Mean (%)*
1	2	3	4	5
2.1	Number Concept	1.4.1	71.3	55.5
2.4	Number Concept	1.4.3.	57.1	50.3
2.2	Number Concept	1.4.4.	35	30
2.3	Number Concept	1.4.5	47.9	37.6
4	Number Concept	1.4.6	54.1	39

Contd

1	2	3	4	5
5.	Addition, Subtraction, Multiplication, Division	2.4.1 2.4.2 2.4.8	70.7	50.2
8.1	Daily Life Problems	3.4.1	42.8	42.7
10.	Daily Life Problems	3.4.14	63.4	63.4
11	Daily Life Problems	3.4.6	22.3	22.3
12	Daily Life Problems	3.4.11	60.6	60.6
13.1	Daily Life Problems	3.4.23	39.4	29.2
14.1	Daily Life Problems	3.4.22	52.4	37
14.2	Daily Life Problems	3.4.24	36	26.5
15	Fractions	4.4.1	71	65.3
16.2	Fractions	4.4.6	39.2	38.5
17	Fractions	4.4.7	17.5	15.4

In two competencies (Speaking – 2.4.1/2.4.3 and Animal Life– 8.3) more than 80% of the children had managed to get some score. However their mean performance was still far from the criterion.

Comparison of Performance of Rural and Urban Children

The sample of the study included children from 50 urban schools and 54 rural schools. Test scores of children from rural and urban schools were compared to see if there was any significant difference in performance. It may be noted here that although the difference in performance between rural and urban children is statistically supported, the mean performance of the entire group ranged between 35% to 48%. The urban children did not perform extraordinarily well.

TABLE 9

Performance of Rural and Urban Children in Hindi, EVS and Arithmetic

	Hindi		*EVS*		*Arithmetic*	
	Rural	Urban	Rural	Urban	Rural	Urban
No. of students	1280	700	1270	719	1270	700
Mean Score	21.25	24.08	17.75	18.80	22.44	21.48
Standard Deviation	9.07	9.31	8.35	7.39	10.79	9.98
't' calculated	–6.74*		–2.92*		2.0	
't' critical = 2.576						

* Significant at $\alpha = 0.01$

It can be seen in Table 9 that the difference between mean scores of urban and rural children was significant on Hindi and EVS. There was no significant difference in the performance on the Arithmetic test.

An explanation for the edge that urban children had over rural children was that urban schools having fixed timings and schedules were still more regular than rural schools. Most teachers lived in the urban areas and hence the probability of their regularity of attendance was higher in the urban system.

Comparison of Girls and Boys

The sample studied constituted both boys and girls. However, there were more boys than girls in the schools, the ratio of boys to girls being 5:4.

There was no significant difference in the performance of boys and girls in Hindi. However, gender differences were observed on EVS and Arithmetic tests with boys performing significantly better than girls (Table 10).

Fig. 3 : Performance of Children in Hindi, EVS and Arithmetic According to Gender

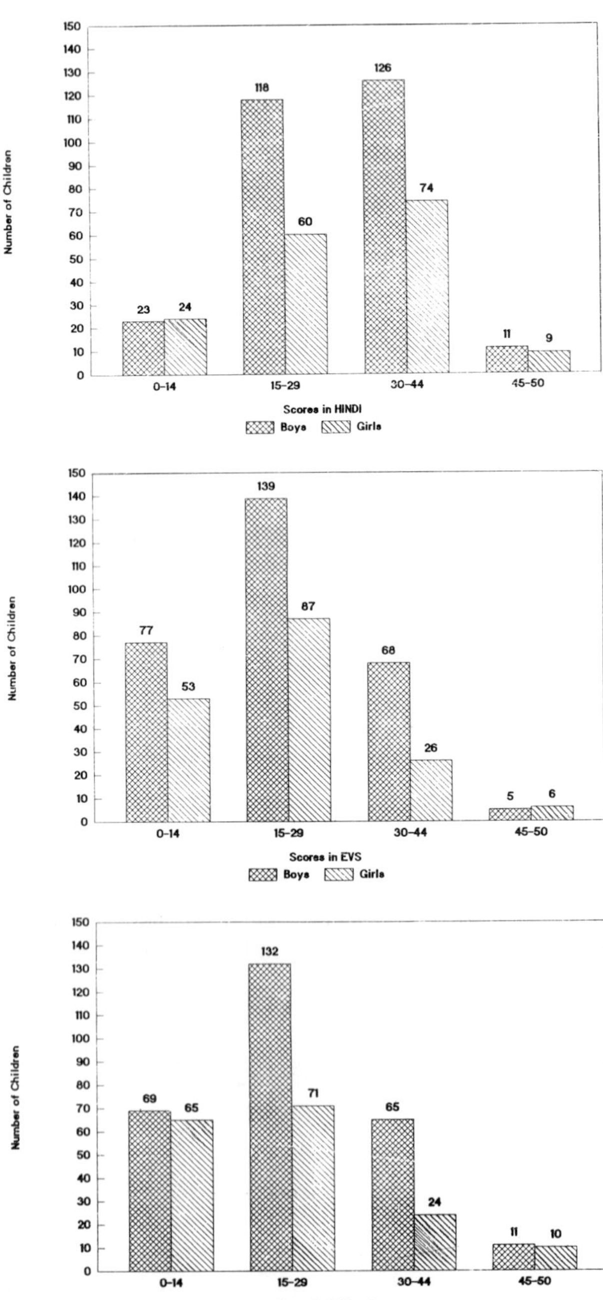

Table 10

Performance of Boys and Girls in Hindi, EVS and Arithmetic

	Hindi		*EVS*		*Arithmetic*	
	Boys	Girls	Boys	Girls	Boys	Girls
No. of children	1083	890	1127	838	1111	851
Mean Score	22.14	22.34	18.55	17.52	23.42	20.37
Standard Deviation	9.13	9.38	8.24	7.73	10.73	9.96
't' calculated	–0.469		2.833*		–6.527	
't' critical - 2.576						

*Significant at $\alpha = 0.01$

It is a well established finding that in the Indian context, societal priorities set for boys and girls are different. As adults, boys are expected to earn a livelihood while girls are expected to be competent in household chores. Their school attendance is often irregular due to their numerous duties at home. Whereas boys are encouraged to study and attend to their school-work, girls receive no such reinforcement and may even be told not to 'waste' time with home work.

This gender bias, observed by the research team, was often reinforced in school in many ways. Teachers themselves attached greater importance to boys' education, and girls were generally socialized to remain quiet and docile.

The fact that the girls were 'as good as boys' in the language test reflects that they had done better in this than in the other two tests. Higher natural ability of girls on language tasks has been a traditional finding across cultures.

School and Teacher Data

The infrastructure and qualitative aspect of a school have a direct bearing on learning and school achievement. Needless to say the characteristics of the teacher are highly salient. Relevant data regarding the physical structure and quality of schools in the sample, and important information about the teaching staff were obtained by interviewing and observing teachers and surveying school facilities.

All the 76 schools* included in the sample had brick buildings. The school buildings usually consisted of one or more rooms, only some with an open verandah. Most facilities such as playground, separate classrooms and schools were in a state of neglect and disrepair. Basic facilities such as playgrounds, separate classrooms and libraries were inadequate (Table 11).

TABLE 11
Infrastructural Facilities Available in Schools (n = 76)

School Data			*Number of Schools*
Location :	(i)	Rural	34
	(ii)	Urban	42
Building type :	(i)	Brick building	76
	(ii)	Tent	0
	(iii)	Barrack	0
Separate Classrooms :	(i)	Available	34
	(ii)	Not available	42
Playground :	(i)	Available	39
	(ii)	Not available	37
Drinking water :	(i)	Available	50
	(ii)	Not available	26
Toilets :	(i)	Available	38
	(ii)	Not available	38
Electricity :	(i)	Available	10
	(ii)	Not available	66
Ventilation :	(i)	Adequate	67
	(ii)	Inadequate	9
Lighting :	(i)	Adequate	59
	(ii)	Inadequate	17
Fan :	(i)	Available	6
	(ii)	Not available	70
Library :	(i)	Available	15
	(ii)	Not available	61

* The sample comprised children from 104 schools. However, school and teacher data were obtained for 76 schools only. In some cases when children from two schools were tested together, data were collected only from the place where actual testing took place.

Drinking water was available only in 50 schools while toilet facilities were there in only about half the schools.

Separate classrooms for different classes were available in 34 schools. The remaining schools were functioning with children of two or more classes (Class III and IV) sitting together in small rooms. Implications of these sparsely equipped schools are clear. The noise level would be high and teachers and students would get distracted easily. Teachers would not have enough space or opportunity to move about and attend to children individually.

A total of 10 schools had electricity and only six had a fan each. While it may be true that many rural children grow up without such basic amenities at home, lack of electricity or fan in the school would mean poor lighting and discomfort. This can be expected to influence attendance and performance of children. Inappropriately designed school buildings and lack of teaching equipment may be factors discouraging regular attendance and children's enthusiasm for school. It is also a reflection of the scant importance given to school, education and the future of children.

The Teachers

The most crucial factor influencing learning and performance in school is the teacher. The teacher's personality, qualifications, experience, training, age and gender are characteristics which would influence the teacher's effectiveness.

Altogether 76 teachers were interviewed, out of which 37 were male and 39 were female. Qualifications ranged from matriculation to post graduation (Table 12). A majority of the teachers were qualified upto matriculation. All the teachers had undergone some training in education such as JBT (Junior Basic Training) or B.Ed. (Bachelor of Education), as a certificate in teacher training is the prerequisite for a teaching job in government schools.

Experience of the teachers in the job ranged from one to 39 years. Most teachers had been in their profession for over 20 years. Many of the teachers interviewed had been teaching in the same school since the beginning of their career.

TABLE 12

Data on Teaching Staff in Schools (n = 76)

Teacher Data			*Number of Teachers*
Age :	(i)	18 – 31 years	1
	(ii)	32 – 45 years	19
	(iii)	Above 45 years	56
Gender :	(i)	Male	37
	(ii)	Female	39
Qualifications :	(:i)	Below Matriculation	5
	(ii)	Matriculation	33
	(iii)	High School (Class 12)	7
	(iv)	Graduation	20
	(v)	Post Graduation	11
Training :	(i)	Junior Basic Training	69
	(ii)	B. Ed.	4
	(iii)	Both (JBT + B. Ed)	3
In-service training :	(i)	Received	16
	(ii)	Not received	60
Experience :	(i)	1– 19 years	14
	(ii)	20 – 39 years	61
	(iii)	40 – 59 years	1
Classes taught :	(i)	Multigrade teaching	31
	(ii)	Only Class V	45
Subjects taught :	(i)	All Subjects	71
	(ii)	Specific Subjects	5
Syllabus:	(i)	Available	39
	(ii)	Not Available	37
Time table :	(i)	Available	55
	(ii)	Not Available	16
	(iii)	Available but not followed	5

In-service training was conspicuous by its absence, with only 16 teachers having received any kind of refresher course or in-service training. This is a defect in the system, for it may lead to complacency on the part of the teacher. Without in-service re-orientation, the educator is in danger of being out of touch with the advances in their own fields of specialization.

A total of 31 teachers were teaching more than one class i.e. doing multigrade teaching, while 45 teachers taught only Class V. Those doing multigrade teaching taught one or two specific subjects to many classes, while the others taught all subjects to a single class.

In several schools, it was observed, that the Headmaster taught Class V. This class is the last stage of the primary level in most U.P. schools. As was customary the highest class got the most important teacher. The Headmaster was expected to help the students 'gear up' to appear for an exam at the end of the year.

It was found that only 39 teachers had a syllabus readily available to them and 55 teachers followed a time-table regularly.

Although provision of minimal facilities in schools and a well-qualified teaching staff are essential for a good educational system, a causative relationship may not necessarily be found between these features and the quality of performance by students.

To study the role of school facilities and teacher characterstics, a sample of high scoring schools and the low scoring schools were compared on these variables. On scrutinizing the mean scores obtained by the students, no relationship could be established between student performance and school infrastructure, or between students performance and teacher qualification. Among those studied, no single factor related to the teachers or schools could be identified as influencing students' performance. A combination of factors made the difference.

The qualitative and intangible aspects of the teaching-learning process, such as motivation of students to learn and teachers' competence in their work also contribute to student achievement.

A view based on the encounters and experiences during the field visit points to the positive role of individual traits of teachers in the

3 to 4 schools where the mean performance of students on all three tests was about 60%. These schools were not well-equipped or spacious. In fact their buildings were typically over-crowded, dingy and dilapidated. The teachers were not more qualified than the others. However, they seemed to have a certain commitment to their work and to the children. School timings and teacher attendance were predictable and regular. The attendance of children was good and they seemed happy at school.

It is known that even the best of facilities and teacher qualifications may not be as strong an indicator as the regularity of the school functioning. Being animated instead of apathetic a teacher is able to elicit a positive response from the students.

6

The Child : A Reflection of the State of Education

The findings of the present study will not shock most people whether educators, planners or tax-payers. People reading newspaper reports like "MP's 75 questions on primary education" in the Times of India (April 14, 1993) or "Deep rot in NDMC Schools" in the Hindustan Times, (Sept. 27, 1992) would say "What else did you expect?" The issue does not elicit strong public reaction partly because the topic is ***education*** and the person at the centre is a **child** from an ***economically disadvantaged*** family.

An Evaluation Method that was Innovative and Replicable

The study had envisaged a method of evaluating children in a way that the assessment was fair to them. To a large extent this objective was achieved due to the rigour observed in the process of developing the test. As the testing procedure shows, the concern for the child was built into this method. By first spending half a day with the children of every school in informal interactions, and subsequently expecting them to answer only one subject booklet each day (lasting about one hour), the quality was not compromised.

In many formal evaluation of young children, especially where examiners are strangers, there would be an element of 'Stranger variable' that can influence results negatively. It was, therefore, of paramount importance that before the children were asked to write out answers, they were in a state of psychological readiness to want to answer.

The friendly and non-threatening stance of the trained researchers further added to making the atmosphere conducive for evaluation. Evidence of this was seen in the fact that the children looked interested in the interactions even on the first day. Their attendance invariably improved on the next day, as the word passed around about "people who play with children". After four days of data collection, when the researchers were leaving, the children's regret was obvious. The format of the booklets resembled story books more than text sheets and generated an interest in children to attempt the problems. An incentive of a pencil to be given to each child on the last day of testing was another reinforcement strategy.

Given these conditions for testing, one may say that the children being tested were predisposed to perform to the best of their ability. Their performance would be a good indicator of their actual academic level. So when the results of Achievement Test analyses showed low achievement levels of children in all the three subjects, the results were considered a realistic assessment of their formal school learning.

The second major aspect of the evaluation model was its replicability. This has implications both for empirical research and classroom evaluation. The need to do continuous evaluation is reiterated in all educational planning. However, there is surprising silence on what the test materials should look like and how these should be presented to children.

Children respond to novel and interesting ways of teaching things by attending to the information given. All that is taught is not necessarily learnt by the child. But when learning occurs in association with a pleasant experience, the child absorbs and remembers it and becomes eager to learn more.

The booklets developed and used in the present study came through as materials that children liked. They spent time looking at the pages with interest. Most of their teachers wanted to retain the booklets for their own future reference. The items had been so selected and designed that teachers would find it possible to make similar items of their own. There were examples of non-stereotypic ways of seeking children's responses to concepts taught in the class.

A related and important finding of the present study that could not be quantified was that, even when simple phenomena in the child's environment were probed through questions in the booklets, most children could not answer satisfactorily (e.g. EVS 4.2 had 13.9% success). It seems that in the teaching process, the children were hardly ever exposed to extrapolation of problem solving from the text-book to real life. Otherwise why would children find it difficult to "list upto five things other than eatables that are derived from plants"?

Derived from this finding it can be said that teachers must demystify knowledge. Knowledge is not what only teachers possess, to be remembered in exact words and reproduced when asked. When knowledge is internalised, it will empower the children to act effectively. Keeping knowledge distant and mysterious may in fact add power to the teacher.

The items in the three booklets are examples of how the standard curriculum can be translated into interesting teaching and evaluation formats and strategies by a teacher. These are replicable. Selecting any one competency, the teacher can make several items so that the pupils grasp the underlying concept. Needless to say, this practice demands flexibility and creativity on the part of teachers. Those who are flexible would like the freedom to prepare the non-conventional formats. Those who believe that these strategies are impractical will require pre-service or an in-service orientation. Renewing their information about children and learning to develop and use materials will follow.

Achievement Levels : A Mirror of the State of Primary Education

The achievement levels of the children of Class V in Hindi, Arithmetic and EVS were in the range of 36% to 45%, being lowest in EVS. The largest number of children scored between 30% and 49%. Similar trends in findings have been reported by Govinda and Varghese (1991) in their study of primary school education in Madhya Pradesh. They had used 80% success as the sole criterion for assessing performance of children in Classes IV and V (N = 2159). In their sample, there were 1419 children from medium to high fee-paying schools. The results showed that only 5% of Class IV and 10% of Class V children in Hindi, and 1% of Class IV and 5% of Class V children in Mathematics had acquired mastery of competencies upto Class IV level. Most of the children achieving this level were from the fee-paying schools, and hence from the middle socio-economic status.

The results of the present study point to a simple conclusion – the children had not acquired the basic elements of the subjects expected to be learnt by the end of class IV, although they were now students of Class V. There are implications in this finding for both teachers and students. It should not be taken to mean that the children could not learn, but that they had not learned. In a general sense, it perhaps confirms what Holt (1982) said about learning in school, *"very little of what is taught in school is learned, very little of what is learned is remembered, very little of what is remembered is used"* (p. 232).

A pedagogical criticism must be levelled at the all too well known inadequacies observed in the school system. The inference can be that teaching was ineffective or that the curriculum inappropriate or the children irregular. The deep structure meaning of this finding, however, is that their schooling had not been able to help children achieve even minimal standards of learning.

Defenders of the system would be quick to point out that the children in the study were, by and large, from economically backward families which are characterised by factors that interfere in the child's education and hence result in low achievement. However, poverty and illiteracy of parents should not be automatically taken as antecedents of poor school performance. The relationship between poverty and competence is not linear. McLoyd (1990) suggested three types of factors that can play a buffering role in neutralising the negative effects of poverty on children's development : (i) parental characteristics; (ii) children's characteristics and (iii) external factors such as extended family support, extra familial figures and the community. Thus, there is not an inevitable determination of outcomes in terms of children's development from the starting point of poverty (Nunes, 1992).

It is much too easy to find an economic argument to explain differences in cognitive performance including school achievement, as research literature would support. But, wherever there has been a concerted effort to create a suitable environment for disadvantaged children, their performance has compared well with that of any other group. The model of education provided by the **Mobile Creches**, a voluntary organisation, is one such example.

The child from a deprived family does not differ in basic intelligence and intelligent behaviour from a child whose family has resources, except when she is severely malnourished. However, her environment may not be conducive to inculcating and promoting school specific learning and so would require different kinds and intensity of inputs from the school. The school has to serve the function of a social support so as to circumvent the effects of poverty at home. Most likely, it has to reach out to the family through the child. It is hypothesized that actions at the child's level can increase self-confidence that will further enhance the child's use of parents and other family members as support and role models (Nunes, 1992). Studies have demonstrated a positive linkage between mass education and economic growth. Returns from primary education are the highest contributors to this linkage among all educational levels (Weiner, 1991).

Teacher attitudes and expectations are known to have an effect on children's perceptions about themselves and school. Teachers influence the child's self esteem and educability through the classroom behavior they knowingly or inadvertently adopt. The impact is greatest during the first few years of school interactions. The strength of teacher expectations was demonstrated in the well-known Rosenthal and Jacobson study (1968).

In the present study, interviews with teachers and observations of their interactions with children revealed that they did not treat children with dignity. The child was low in the hierarchy. Power assertions through punishment, humiliation and ridicule was common. Verbal remarks to children or about them conveyed that the teachers viewed children as a different kind of species from themselves. Teachers in turn, are viewed as objects of awe and fear by the children.

Student-teacher relationships with such overtones cannot be conducive for creating a learning environment. Commenting on teacher-student communication in the classroom, Elkind (1979) wrote, "Children are least like us in their thoughts but most like us in their feelings" (p. 151). Adults often expect children to understand all that they say, but not to share the same feelings. As adults we like to believe that there is a close relation between thought and feeling, and would feel justified in saying, "I am too sad to be able to solve this problem"., If thinking is influenced by feeling, all teacher-pupil interactions must take this into account. To address this issue the 'cognitive' curricula do not need an 'affective' curriculum as an added new mode of interaction. What must be done is that the existing teacher-pupil interaction be made more positive. Once children begin to feel that they are worthy of an adult's liking and respect, they feel good about themselves and confident about their abilities to learn in a variety of domains. "At the heart of the affective interactions between teacher and child is the teacher's conception of the child" (Elkind, 1979, p. 153). ***We need pre-service and in-service teacher training programmes designed to give teachers a better understanding of child development.***

A close scrutiny of the results in Tables 5, 6 and 7 reveals that the items or areas in which the children's scores were the lowest we were those that required definite teacher input and could not have been learned by children through incidental learning. For example, in Hindi these were areas of Reading, Speaking (describing a picture orally,) and Writing (a guided composition). In EVS the questions on Energy Use, Plant Life, Means of Communication, Solar and Lunar Eclipse and Map Skills were in this category. In Arithmetic too, wherever the problem required application of the basic operations, the performance was low. Understanding of fractions was the weakest among all arithmetical operations.

These findings, despite the low scores of children, go in their favour. It seems that most of what they could answer correctly (apart from basic literacy and numeracy) they had imbibed from their out-of-school experiences and as a function of maturation. The competencies that ought to develop as a result of teaching in Class IV were generally not a part of their repertoire.

As is evident from the research design of the study, the children had not been given time to prepare for the 'Tests', something that they would normally do for their school examinations. This was a deliberate step as the attempt was to explore what concepts children had acquired at the end of four years of schooling rather than what they could memorize. It was their competence in specific academic areas that had to be assessed and not simply short-term memory. The fact that achievement levels were low must not be seen as on indicator of inferior cognitive competence of the children. Performance is mediated by many factors other than competence. In the case of school performance, these would include several variables related to home, school and teachers.

Theories of Piaget and Montessori have important implications for classroom practice. Both had extended the argument of the ability of the child for ***self-regulation*** to education (Eklind, 1979). By self-regulation is meant direction and organization from within.

Whether or not a child's self-regulated activity will be optimized for positive ends will depend upon his or her past history and upon the environmental circumstances. Every classroom practice presupposes a particular conception about children and how they learn. Their behaviour is not a fixed expression of their genotype or social class, but can change with new environmental circumstances. It means that children can learn self-regulation, but it also means that they can unlearn it, depending upon their experiences.

In young children, whether at school or at home, self-related activities should be emphasized to a greater extent than other learning modes. The teachers must be able to devise methods by which children themselves feel in control of their learning.

Another component of Piagetian theory useful for application in education is that, compared to an adult, the child is a ***cognitive alien*** (Elkind, 1979). This means that children do not think in the same way as adults do and this is not wrong or bad, it is simply different or alien.

From a classroom point of view, it means that adults should not take anything for granted insofar as the child's knowledge or understanding is concerned. According to Elkind, "This is the single most difficult rule for teachers to acquire and, once acquired, to abide by. Failure to follow this rule is, perhaps, the most important cause of ineffective teaching practice " (p. 147).

In no way does it mean that one has to talk down to children or be condescending to them. On the contrary one has to relate to children as one would to intelligent individuals in another country. That means, we have to try hard to find out what they know and how they comprehend reality, in order to establish a basis of communication and to learn where to begin instructions. Often teachers demonstrate ***instructional egocentrism,*** that is, failure to assess the level of understanding before proceeding with instructions.

Decades ago, Montessori had devised materials and methods based on the principle of "Child first, method later". Set in our system of education today, we put the need for new methods ahead of careful observation of the child. "The price of effective teaching is constant observation" (Elkind, p. 148).

Child-Curriculum Match

The government schools in U.P. were using textbooks based on syllabi and content prescribed by NCERT and the State Education Department. Such homogenized content perhaps cannot do justice to the diverse ethnic, cultural, linguistic and demographic backgrounds to which children belong. The content of lessons and the style in which these are taught often do not match the child's home and ecology. For example, it is developmentally appropriate for 10 year olds to learn to read maps and draw simple maps. However, children should first be introduced to the concept of plotting their immediate neighbourhoods and the village or urban neighbourhood in a map format before the concept of the map of India and its States is introduced.

The item on map skills in the EVS booklet was based on one of the MLL Competencies of class III related to map reading. Yet the children's success was only 10.3%. Needless to say, children were not at all familiar with such exercises. Apart from the content, the print, the format and drawings in the books were of poor quality, making them unattractive for young children.

The learning environment and the child must find an appropriate match. Educational environments need to be geared to the socio-cultural ethos of the child, with the teaching of unfamiliar concepts being an exception and not the rule. These could be included for novelty and challenge to the child's mind. Contents of text books and work-books need to be made not culture-free but culture-friendly for the child in every school.

Another variable in the child-curriculum match is the medium of instruction in school. Even though U.P. is a Hindi speaking State and formal teaching is known to be done in Hindi, there seemed to be a problem in the use of Hindi as it was spoken formally and as it was taught and assessed. Children in different regions of U.P. were found to use Hindi dialects that were quite different in their sounds and intonations compared to standard Hindi. Semantic differences were also noticed in their speech. This means that children experienced the language of instruction as a little different from their own.

This could bear heavily on the educability of children. Language being the most crucial factor in the comprehension and expression of academic material, unfamiliar linguistic styles of textbooks can place a child at a disadvantage. The point that needs attention once again is related to the primacy of the child over the content of education. While learning the language of the educated society is certainly a desirable goal of education, at the primary stage, it is more important that the child develops knowledge of the world around her in her own language. She must find answers to her numerous questions in an effortless mode. Later she can learn that language also has aspects that need to be mastered.

Evaluation Against MLLs

One of the paradigms used to develop test items in the present study was the MLL concept as stated in the document "Minimum Levels of Learning at Primary Stage' (NCERT, 1991). The analysis of children's performance in these items showed that mastery level (i.e. 80% success by 80% children) was not seen in any competency (Tables 8a, b & c). However, above 50% performance was shown by more than 50% of children.

This data can be useful in knowing bench-mark levels of children in U.P. schools if any intervention is planned. Similarly low standards of performance were also reported by Govinda and Varghese (1991) in schools in Madhya Pradesh. However, in both the studies while children did not have 'competencies' required to be attained by Class V, there were all in class V. The reason is that while the children are evaluated against the standard of 30% performance to promote them to next class, the MLL norm has been fixed at 80% level of performance. This 50% gap is too large to be filled by an improvement in the quality of basic education.

The minimum level needs to be made more realistic and hence brought down to perhaps 50% performance by 80% children. The upper range of performance to be aimed at could be 80% and above. A range is necessary in keeping with the variations in competence and performance levels of children and teachers. Success at lower minimum levels could serve as a stepping stone towards the next level. If anything short of 80% success is perceived as failure, it would interfere in the maintenance of a high level of motivation among teachers and children.

The MLL document should be reviewed critically as there are other dimensions of this approach that appear as though considerations for individual differences among children have been neglected. In delineating learning tasks, it is implied that, for a particular 'input' given to students, a set of 'learning outcomes' will be generated. The child appears to be equated to a machine in this model.

Another criticism of the MLL approach advanced by Kumar (1992) is that it erases the possibility of a holistic view of educational aims by dividing everything into competencies and sub-competencies. Pointing out problems in interpreting the 'competencies', Kumar picked up an example from Grade II. It states that "the child should identify important public places such as school, panchayat-ghar etc. in the locality and know their importance ' (2.2.1). He commented, "It is fine to expect a child's familiarity with these institutions, but how do we expect the child to demonstrate her acknowledgement of their importance? The assumption seems to be that the teacher will prompt children to write cliches like 'the panchayat symbolises rural self-reliance' and so on".

Education of the Girl in School

We have come to expect gender differences in almost all spheres. The findings of the present study show better performance of boys in EVS and Arithmetic. The results also confirm the fact that fewer girls than boys attend school. One of the implications is that the education system has not been able to break into the bias against the female child. Her socialization in the family and its effect on her access to educational facilities are common knowledge.

In last few years policy makers are being influenced by research on women that shows that there are strong linkages between women's schooling and their reproductive and maternal behaviour (Jain & Nag 1987; Le Vine et al., 1991). If girls go to school but drop out before completing primary education (before acquiring minimum reading and numerical skills), they lack skills to assimilate information disseminated through the mass media, especially through printed materials. They are slower in shifting to the requisite fertility regulating and child care techniques.

With regard to maternal behaviour, mothers with more schooling express a greater desire for further education, higher occupational aspirations for their children, lower expectations of material returns from them, greater exposure to the media, and a greater tendency to view young infants as capable of communication. All these are attitudes that give promise of a better future for all children.

The Rural-Urban Difference

In this study, it was found that rural schools were operating as 'neighbourhood school' where children from a range of abilities and socio-economic levels attended the same school. The urban school, in our sample, was frequently the last resort for an urban family. The privatised educational system was the preferred choice and only those who could not afford the tuition fees or who did not wish to spend on it, sent their children to the Municipal Schools.

There was thus a feeling that the rural schools were a little more advantaged. But there was one big difference : the rural schools were more irregular, being closed when the teacher was not available for any reason. The hours of work were also unpredictable. Teachers generally lived in urban areas and travelled to the rural schools. Since the urban schools were closer, the absenteeism of teachers and the closing of schools was less noticeable in the urban area. On the whole therefore, the performance of children from the urban schools, was better than that of rural children although both levels were quite low.

7

Epilogue : Sharing Our Insights with the Reader

Whenever a research report has been completed it has been the practice in our Department (Child Development, Lady Irwin College) to discuss what did not go into the report. The unwritten part has incidental observations and first person accounts of the humour and pathos of the human condition,. Inferences cannot be based on a single episode – on this the research code is inviolable – and those do not get written up, except occasionally as a Post Script or an After Thought. A decision was made by this project team to record the invisible findings and the over-extended conclusions leaving their acceptance to the discretion of the reader.

Children

Children are active learners, constantly seeking to know, to comprehend, to master; seeking also to give and receive affection and trust. Poverty, per se, is not related to the child's exploratory or epistemic behaviour, but it does have indirect effects in reducing (a) the child's energy and attention levels and (b) the school's attitude to the child's educability.

Natural resilience enables children to cope with a variety of situations and to gain something from every experience. The benefits of schooling appeared to be marginally higher for girls.

Teachers

The country needs dedicated teachers to the same extent that it needs dedicated bus conductors, athletes or accountants. In other words, dedication helps any job to be done better, but there is no reason to attach the adjective especially to teachers. Teachers must have both the knowledge and the technique to impart it appropriately. Empathy for children is the invisible attribute of a good teacher, but it is a characteristic that is not easily objectified, at the time of recruitment. Children are quick to identify an empathetic adult, but they are not usually consulted. Not the teacher's education, training or experience **by itself** seemed to be a good predictor for children's learning achievement, as much as the teacher's willingness to be in the classroom and his regularity.

Methods

There is no simple 'best' method for teaching young children the basics of literacy and numeracy. There is however a variety of good methods from which the teacher can choose, for each situation, afresh. There are some criteria of methods that apply across the board.

They are (a) comprehensibility for children (b) coherence with the content and (c) capability for use in the Panchayat/Municipal School system. Used with a little imagination and with concern for the child's education, the variations of method will emerge in the course of classroom activity. Using a wider range of resources, including those of the community will add to effective teaching.

Texts

This term is used in the literal rather than the metaphoric sense. What is contained in the text is part of the formal knowledge system – everything else is not defined as "knowledge". A great deal of improvement is called for in the text books used at the primary level. They are usually written by people out of touch with children and the way they think and feel. Quite often the text books serve as propaganda for the State, the region or the culture. The content could alternatively be "morally uplifting" or "patriotic". But more than all these aspects, is the fact that the school text is treated in the same way a religious text is treated by fundamentalists. Nothing can be changed in the slightest and must be learnt by rote as indicative of the reverence for infallible knowledge.

Context

(a) For the text : In order to provide material that is relevant to all children, the textual material is often context-free. Such an approach may help in the teaching of numeracy – but it cannot be considered suitable for young children. One needs context-sensitive and context-specific writing. Given the diversity in socio-economic and cultural settings, we need a variety of contexts, not only the child's own, with which she is familiar.

(b) For the learning experience : The context of the classroom, the space, the lighting, ventilation, furniture, black board, bulletin boards, play areas, safety, noise level and play and learning equipment available – all these are different constituents of the settings. No single factor is directly influencing children's achievement and a holistic rather than a reductionist explanation seems to be called for, regarding the context of education.

The System

Where a school has only one teacher, teaching several levels is a factor that becomes difficult to handle. The sense of isolation of the only teacher in the rural school is a real one. However, even when a few teachers are appointed to one school, the lack of a supervisory mechanism is obvious.

Even an ordinary school with a routine schedule and pompous text books is able to provide a setting, for the child to learn. There is no denying that improving the quality of the school enhances learning and the child's joy and self-esteem. But even a minimally equipped school which functions with regularity achieves more than is normally credited to it.

Evaluation

This was the core aspect of the study – to develop suitable

methods to check if literacy and numeracy of Class-V level had been reached by children in Municipal and Panchayat Schools in U.P. In this connection, the newly launched Minimal Levels of Learning (MLL) was being treated by many as a panacea for the inadequacies of the education of several million school children in the country. While it helped the teacher to break up the curriculum into micro-units, it could get over-emphasised as 'real knowledge' and become counter-productive to understanding the relationships between things.

In some cases, it was felt by our team that the M in MLL could have stood for Maximal rather than Minimal. Setting a level of 80% attainment by 80% of the children as a criterion measure took the MLL out of the range of feasibility. There is a risk of children being twice damned as failures – once in the regular exam and once in the MLL. These comments refer to the 1991 version of the NCERT document. It is possible that the large number of teams working on the MLLs have subsequently modified the items and made them more appropriate.

A final comment : it is possible to make evaluation more imaginative, more acceptable to children, more flexible and less frightening : but testing cannot be a substitute for teaching. That challenging task is the most important one. It can be made more rewarding and more exciting by helping teachers to see that children are keen learners when allowed to function with self-esteem.

S. Anandalakshmy

References

Bartwal, H.S. (1992). Deep rot in NDMC schools. ***The Hindustan Times.*** 27th September.

Chitnis, S. (1987). Education and social stratification : an illustration from a metropolitan city. In R. Ghosh & M. Zachariah (Eds.). ***Education and the process of change.*** New Delhi: Sage Publications.

Department of Education. (1986). ***Programme of action-National policy on education.*** New Delhi : Department of Education, Ministry of Human Resource Development, Government of India.

Entwisle, D.R. (1975). Language behaviour and educability. In M.L. Maehr & W.M. Stallings (Eds.), ***Culture, child and school.*** California Brooks/Cole Publishing Co.

Elkind, D. (1979). ***The child and society.*** New York : Oxford University Press.

Ghosh, R. & Zachariah, M. (1987). ***Education and the process of change.*** New Delhi : Sage Publications.

Govinda, R. & Varghese, V.N. (1991). ***The quality of basic educational services in India (Draft Report).*** New Delhi : National Institute of Educational Planning and Administration.

Holt, J. (1982). ***How children fail.*** England : Pelican Books.

Holt J. (1990). ***Learning all the time.*** England : Pelican Books.

Illich, I. (1971). ***Deschooling society***. Great Britain : Penguin Books.

Illich, I. (1972). Breakdown of schools. ***Seminar,*** October.

Jain, A.K. & Nag. M. (1987). Importance of female literacy reduction. In R. Ghosh & M. Zachariah (Eds.), ***Education and the process of***

change. New Delhi : Sage Publications.

Kamii, C. & Kamii, M. (1990). Why achievement testing should stop. In C. Kamii (Ed.), ***Achievement testing in the early grades.*** Washington D.C. : National Association for the Education of Young Children.

Kapoor, A. (1993).. MPs' 75 questions on primary education. ***Times of India,*** 14th April.

Kumar, K. (1992). Discarded technique finds way into curriculum. ***Times of India.*** 9th August.

LeVine R.A., Levine S.E., Richman A., Uribe M.T., Correa C.S., & Miller P.M. (1991). Women's schooling and child care in the demographic transition : a Mexican case study. ***Population and Development Review*** 17, No. 3, September.

McLoyd. V.C. (1990). The impact of economic hardship on Black families and children : psychological distress, parenting and socio-emotional development. ***Child Development, 61, 311-346.***

National Council of Educational Research and Training. (1991). ***Minimum levels of learning at the primary stage.*** New Delhi : NCERT.

National Council of Educational Research and Training: (1986). ***Fifth educational survey of India.*** New Delhi : NCERT.

Nunes, T. (1992). ***The environment of the child.*** Paper prepared for the Bernard van Leer Foundation. The Hague : Bernard van Leer Foundation.

Rogers, C. (1983). ***Freedom to learn for the 80s.*** Columbia : Charles E. Merrill Publishing Co.

Rosenthal, R., & Jacobson, L. (1968). ***Pygmalion in the classroom.*** New York : Holt, Rinehart and Winston.

Weiner, M. (1991). ***The child and the state in India.*** Delhi : Oxford University Press.

Appendix-I

Practice Items Used with Children Prior to Achievement Testing

Before administering the Achievement Tests, one day in each school was spent practicing items similar to those in the test booklets with the children. The practice session started after talking to the children,, taking their heights and weights and only when it was felt that the children were comfortable with the researchers. The items used during this session are given below. Each item was preceded by a discussion wherein the underlying concept and the format of the example was explained to the children. For example – the item on 'Ascending and Descending Order' was introduced by asking children what was meant by the terms : arranging in order, ascending and descending. A concrete task was given to the children. Five children were asked to come forward and stand in order of increasing height and then decreasing height.

Another illustration was done by asking 5-6 children their age. They were asked to sit in order of increasing and then decreasing age. If it was felt that the children had understood the concept, then an example using numbers was solved on the blackboard (Item No. 1 given below). This procedure was followed with all the items. After completing the example a practice booklet was given to each child, to solve individually.

1. अकों को क्रम में लिखना :

   12, 15, 9, 8, 20

   बढ़ते क्रम में

   घटते क्रम में

2. प्रत्येक संख्या में 8 का स्थानीय मान बताओ :

   81 में 8 का स्थानीय मान 8 ☐ है ।

   8520 में 8 का स्थानीय मान 8 ☐ है ।

3. हल करो :

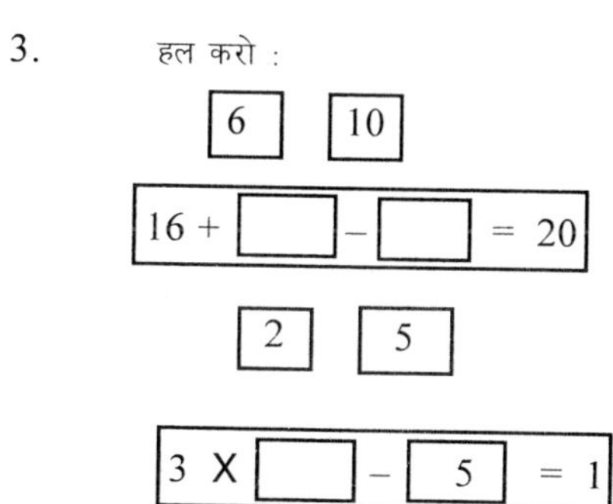

4. हल करो :

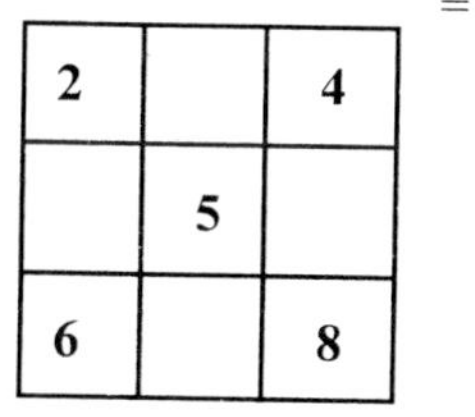

5. गुणज
2 के गुणज बताओ ।

चालाक बंदर

एक बार एक बंदर को जंगल में एक झोला पड़ा मिल गया । उस झोले में एक कंघा और शीशा था । कंघे और शीशे को देखकर बंदर अचम्भे में पड़ गया । उसकी समझ में नहीं आ रहा था कि ये दोनों चीजें किस काम आती हैं ।

काफी देर बाद उसकी समझ में आया कि शीशे का मुँह जिसके सामने हो जाता है उसी की सूरत शीशे में दिखाई पड़ती है । बंदर बड़ा चालाक था । उसने सोचा अब तो मैं इसके द्वारा किसी को भी वश में कर सकता हूँ । यह सोचकर वह शान से अकड़ता हुआ चल पड़ा ।

बंदर को अकड़ता देखकर जंगल के शेर से न रहा गया । उसने पूछा 'क्यों रे, बंदर की तरह नहीं चलते बनता ?' 'अकड़ता हुआ क्यों न चलूँ , क्या मैं किसी से कम हूँ ।" बंदर ने जवाब दिया ।

यह सुनकर शेर ने और गुस्से में आकर कहा, "अकड़ के बच्चे, जाता है या लगाऊँ दो चपत ?"

बंदर भी इस बार तनकर बोला, 'अरे जा-जा, तू क्या चपत लगाएगा, तेरे जैसों को तो मैं मुट्ठी में बंद करके झोले में रखता हूँ !

यह सुनकर शेर गुस्से से तमतमा उठा और बोला, "दिखा तो कहाँ हैं, मेरे जैसे तेरे झोले में।" इतना कहकर वह बंदर की ओर मारने को बढ़ा ।

बन्दर ने तुरन्त जवाब दिया, "नहीं मानता तो देख" और ऐसा कह कर झोले से शीशा निकाल कर शेर के सामने रख दिया । शेर को वास्तव में बंदर के हाथ एक शेर दिखाई पड़ा । वह अपनी ही तस्वीर को दूसरा शेर समझकर सोचने लगा कि ज़रूर ही कोई बलशाली बंदर है, इससे लड़ाई मोल लेना अच्छा नहीं ।

तुरन्त शेर बन्दर से नम्र भाव से बोला, 'श्रीमानजी, आपसे हमारी क्या लड़ाई ?' बंदर ने शीशे को झोले में रखा और पहले की भांति अकड़ता हुआ चला गया ।

6. कहानी सुनकर प्रश्न का उत्तर दो ।

सही उत्तर के आगे [✓] का चिन्ह लगाओ ।

यह कहानी किसके बारे में थी ।

- बन्दर और चिड़िया [ ]
- शेर और लोमड़ी [ ]
- भालू और शेर [ ]
- बन्दर और शेर [ ]

APPENDIX II

Practice Booklet

लेडी इर्विन कॉलेज, नई दिल्ली

Paradigms for Evaluating Primary Education

नाम :

आयु : लड़का/लड़की

गाँव/शहर :

स्कूल :

कक्षा :

हिन्दी

1. अभी तुमने "चालाक बंदर" कहानी सुनी। उससे सम्बन्धित प्रश्नों के उत्तर दो।
सही उत्तर के सामने ✓ का चिन्ह लगाओ।

1.1 बंदर को जंगल में क्या मिला ?

- ट्रंक मिला ☐
- झोला मिला ☐
- डिब्बा मिला ☐
- बोतल मिली ☐

1.2 बंदर को झोले में क्या मिला ?

- रोटी व सब्जी मिली ☐
- चश्मा व कलम मिली ☐
- कंघा व शीशा मिला ☐
- कंकड़ व पत्थर मिले ☐

2. इस कहानी में आगे क्या हुआ होगा ? अपने मन से दो वाक्यों में लिखो।

पर्यावरण अध्ययन

1. पाचन में हमारे शरीर के जो अंग कार्य करते हैं उन पर घेरा लगाओ।

अमाशय (पेट),	हृदय,	कान,	मुँह,	नाक,	आंत,
		खाद्य-नलिका			

2. रेखा खींच कर दिए गए पदार्थों को उनके गुणों से मिलाओ।

जल	• जल का ठोस रुप है
केरोसीन	• आसानी से टूट जाता है
बर्फ	• रंगहीन है
रबड़	• जलने में सहायक है
कांच	• आसानी से मुड़ जाता है

गणित

1. नीचे लिखी संख्याओं को क्रम में लिखो :

   40, 29, 38, 56, 45

   बढ़ते क्रम में :

   घटते क्रम में :

2. प्रत्येक संख्या में २ का स्थानीय मान लिखो :

   261 में 2 का स्थानीय मान 2 [ ] है।

   2354 में 2 का स्थानीय मान 2 [ ] है।

3. नीचे दिए गए सवाल हल करो। [ ] में लिखे अंकों को सही स्थान में लिखो।

   [2] [5]

   10 + [ ] - [ ] = 13

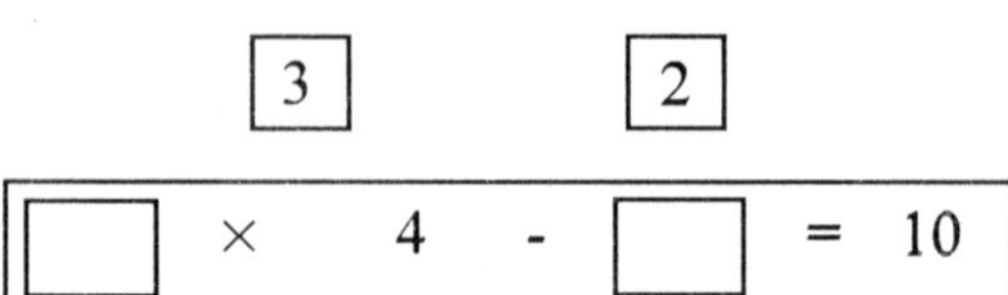

4. नीचे बने वर्ग में अंक भरकर जादुई वर्ग बनाओ। याद रहे हरेक पंक्ति का जोड़ बराबर हो।

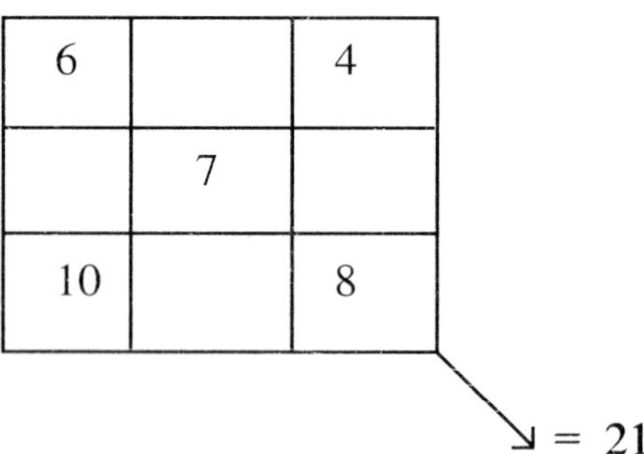

5. नीचे बने वर्ग में **4** के गुणज पर घेरा लगाओ।

1	2	3	4	5	6	7	8	9	10
11	12	13	14	15	16	17	18	19	20
21	22	23	24	25	26	27	28	29	30
31	32	33	34	35	36	37	38	39	40
41	42	43	44	45	46	47	48	49	50
51	52	53	54	55	56	57	58	59	60
61	62	63	64	65	66	67	68	69	70
71	72	73	74	75	76	77	78	79	80
81	82	83	84	85	86	87	88	89	90
91	92	93	94	95	96	97	98	99	100

Appendix-IIIa

'बूझो तो जानें – १' के लिए अनुदेश

१. पहली पहेली है 'सुनो और करो' । इस पहेली के दो भाग हैं । प्रत्येक भाग दो बार पढ़कर बच्चों को सुनाएँ । पहला भाग पूर्ण होने पर ही दूसरा हल करने को दीजिए । बच्चों को यह समझाना होगा कि वे प्रत्येक पहेली को ध्यान से सुनने के पश्चात् ही उसे हल करें।

इस पहेली में केवल रंगीन पेंसिल का प्रयोग करें। पहेली शुरू करने से पहले सभी बच्चों को रंगीन पेंसिल दीजिए। ध्यान दें कि कोई बच्चा फुटपट्टी का प्रयोग न करें ।

'सुनो और करो'

नीचे लिखे वाक्यों का प्रयोग करके बच्चों को निर्देश दें ।

(क) "तीन तिकोन बनाओ । पहले तिकोन में रंग भरो, दूसरे को खाली छोड़ो और तीसरे में बिंदियाँ लगाओ ।"

(ख) "एक चौकोर बनाओ । इसमें चार पंखुड़ियों वाला एक फूल बनाओ । फूल के दो पत्ते भी बनाओ । केवल इन दो पत्तों में रंग भरो ।"

पहली पहेली पूर्ण होने पर बच्चों को पुस्तिका बन्द करने के लिए कहें ।

२. **अगली दो पहेलियाँ (नं० २ और ३) एक कविता पर आधारित है । बच्चों से कहें,**

"अब तुम एक कविता सुनोगे । कविता का शीर्षक है 'बाँसुरी वाला' इस कविता को ध्यान से सुनो क्योंकि तुम्हें इससे सम्बन्धित कुछ पहेलियाँ हल करनी हैं।"

बाँसुरी वाला

'बात सात सौ साल पुरानी
सुनो ध्यान से प्यारे
जयपुर नामक एक शहर था
रावी नदी किनारे ।

यूँ तो शहर बहुत सुन्दर था
जयपुर जिसका नाम
मगर वहॉ के लोगों का
हो गया था चैन हराम ।

दुबले चूहे, मोटे चूहे
लम्बे चूहे, छोटे चूहे
उपर नीचे, आगे पीछे
जिधर भी देखो चूहे ।

बाहर चूहे, घर में चूहे
दरवाजे और दर में चूहे
खिड़की और आलों में चूहे
थालों और प्यालों में चूहे।

क्या ट्रंक और सन्दूक में चूहे ?
फौजी की बन्दूक में चूहे,
अफसर की गाड़ी में चूहे,
नौकर की दाढ़ी में चूहे ।

चूहों से घबराकर
राजा ने किया ऐलान,
जो उन से पीछा छुटवाए
पाए ढेर ईनाम ।

सुनकर ये ऐलान वहाँ पर
पहुँचा एक मदारी
लाल कलंदर नाम था उसका
मुँह पर लम्बी दाढ़ी ।

झोले से बंसी निकालकर
मीठी तान बजाई
जिसको सुनकर चूहा-सेना
दौड़ी-दौड़ी आई ।

आगे-आगे चला मदारी
पीछे चूहे सारे
चलते चलते वो जा पहुँचे
रावी नदी किनारे ।

ले गया मदारी सब चूहों को
रावी नदी के अंदर
एक भी जिन्दा नहीं बचा
सब डूबे नदी के अन्दर ।

इसके पश्चात् बच्चों को अपनी पुस्तिकाओं में कविता से सम्बंधित पहेलियों को हल करने के लिए कहिए ।

श्रुतलेख

पहेली ४ के लिए बच्चों को 'बासुँरी वाला' कविता के निम्नलिखित पदों का श्रुतलेख करवाएँ । प्रत्येक पंक्ति दो बार पढ़ें ।

क्या, ट्रंक और संदूक में चूहे ?
फौजी की बन्दूक में चूहे,
अफसर की गाड़ी में चूहे,
नौकर की दाढ़ी में चूहे ।

चूहों से घबराकर
राजा ने किया ऐलान,
जो उनसे पीछा छुटवाए
पाए ढेर ईनाम ।

४. **पहेली नं १३ के लिए निदेश**

इस पहेली को मौखिक रूप से हल करना है । इस क्रिया के लिए दिया हुआ चित्र, टेप रिकॉर्डर व कैसेट की आवश्यकता है । यह एक वैयक्तिक प्रश्न है, इसलिए प्रत्येक बच्चे को एक - एक करके अलग स्थान में / समूह से दूर / बुलाएँ ; ध्यान रखें कि बच्चा आराम से बैठा हो । चित्र दिखाकर निर्देश दें :

"दिए गए चित्र को ध्यान से देखो । इस चित्र में क्या दिखाई दे रहा है ? इस चित्र में क्या हो रहा है, कहानी बनाकर बताओ ।"

यदि बच्चा बोल न पाए या हिचकिचाए तो प्रश्न दोहराएँ और उसे बोलने के लिए प्रोत्साहित करें, परन्तु, स्वयं कोई उत्तर न दें । जैसे ही बच्चा बोलना शुरू करे उसके उत्तर को रिकार्ड करना शुरू करें । इसका महत्व यह है कि आप बच्चे की ओर ध्यान दे सकते हैं व आप को उसका उत्तर उसी समय लिखना नहीं पड़ेगा ।

Appendix-III b

Achievement Test

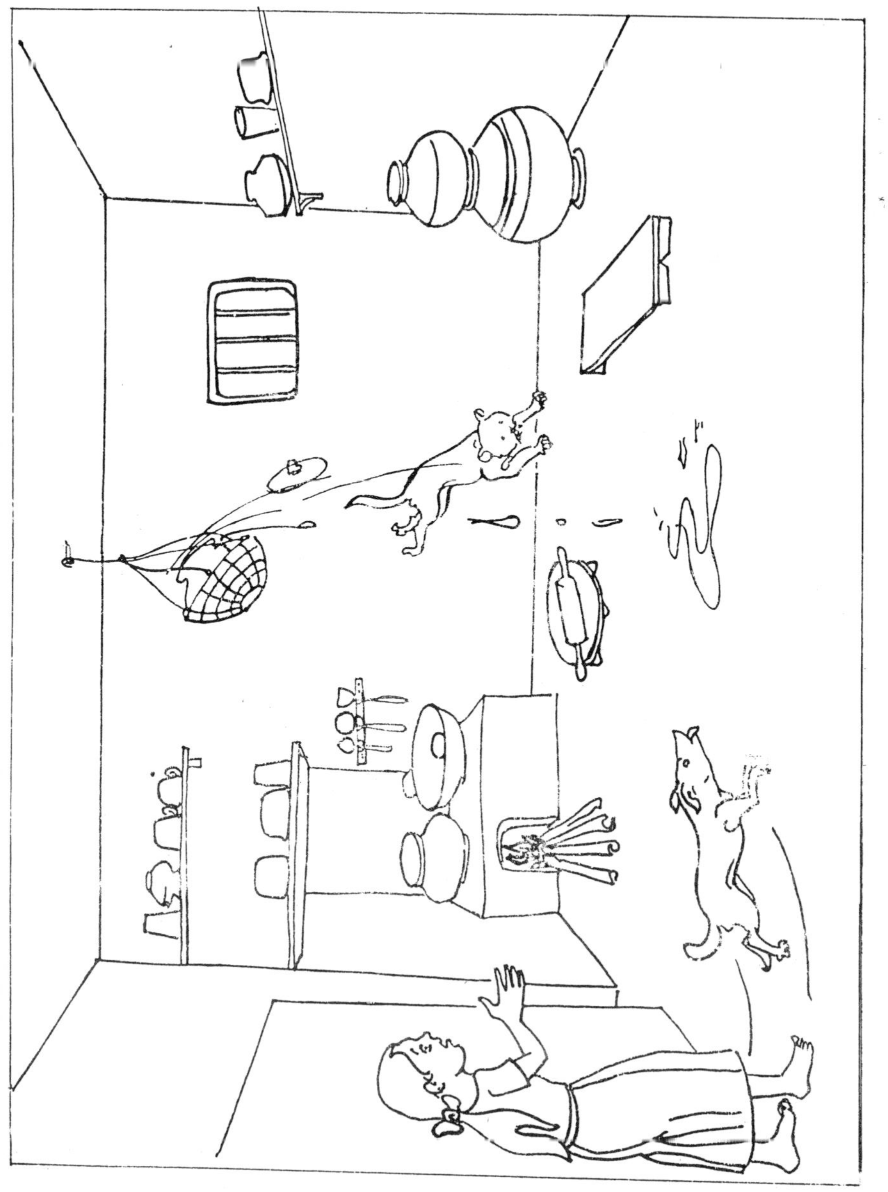

बूझो
तो
जानें - 1

लेडी इर्विन कॉलेज, नई दिल्ली

Paradigms for Evaluating Primary Education

हिन्दी

नाम :

आयु : लड़का/लड़की

गाँव/शहर :

स्कूल :

कक्षा :

1	3.3	7	9.3	1.1
2	4	8	9.4	12
3.1	5	9.1	9.5	13
3.2	6	9.2	10	

दिनांक :

अवधि :

परीक्षक :

लेडी इर्विन कॉलेज, नई दिल्ली
Paradigms for Evaluating Primary Education

हिन्दी

नाम :

आयु : लड़का/लड़की

गाँव/शहर :

स्कूल :

कक्षा :

1	3.3	7	9.3	11
2	4	8	9.4	12
3.1	5	9.1	9.5	13
3.2	6	9.2	10	

दिनांक :

अवधि :

परीक्षक :

2. अभी तुमने "बाँसुरी वाला" कविता सुनी । उससे सम्बन्धित प्रश्नों के उत्तर दो ।

रिक्त स्थान भरो ।

(i) कविता में शहर का नाम ------------ था ।

(ii) यह शहर -------------- नदी के किनारे था ।

(iii) मदारी का नाम --------------- था ।

(iv) मदारी के --------------- बजाने से सब

---- भागे और ------------- के अंदर कूद गए ।

3. सही उत्तर के सामने [✓] का चिन्ह लगाओ । पहले उदाहरण देखो ।

शहर के लोगों का परेशानी से छुटकारा किसने दिलवाया ?

-- चूहों ने [ ]

-- मदारी ने [✓]

-- अफसर ने [ ]

-- नौकर ने [ ]

3.1 शहर के लोग परेशान थे क्योंकि :

-- शहर नदी किनारे था । ☐

-- शहर बहुत सुन्दर था । ☐

-- शहर में बहुत अधिक चूहे थे । ☐

-- शहर में मदारी आया था । ☐

○○○

3.2 शहर के लोगों की परेशानी कैसे दूर हुई ?

-- दरवाज़े खोल देने से । ☐

-- फौजी के बन्दूक चलाने से । ☐

-- सन्दूक बन्द कर देने से । ☐

-- मदारी के बाँसुरी बजाने से । ☐

○○○

3.3 परेशानी से छुटकारा दिलवाने के लिए शहर में ऐलान किसने करवाया था ।

-- नौकर ने ☐

-- राजा ने ☐

-- फौजी ने ☐

-- अफसर ने ☐

○○○

4. अब तुम "बाँसुरी वाला" कविता में से दो पदों के **श्रुतलेख** के लिए तैयार हो जाओ । नीचे का स्थान प्रयोग करो ।

श्रुतलेख

5. **समान अर्थ का खेल :**

अहमद और गोपाल दो दोस्त हैं । उन्हें एक खेल खेलना पसन्द है । जब अहमद कोई शब्द बोलता है तो गोपाल उस के समान अर्थ वाला कोई दूसरा शब्द बोलता है ।

जैसे :-- अहमद बोला--"जल" तो गोपाल ने झट से कहा--"पानी" ।

नीचे कुछ शब्द दिए हैं जो अहमद ने बोले थे । गोपाल ने क्या उत्तर दिए होंगे ?

अहमद बोला -	**गोपाल ने उत्तर दिया** -
जल	पानी
(i) धन	--------------------
(ii) वायु	--------------------
(iii) आकाश	--------------------
(iv) पर्वत	--------------------
(v) धरती	--------------------

6. दिए गए शब्दों के **विलोम शब्द** लिखो । फिर उन्हें वर्ग में भरो ।

	विलोम शब्द
सफलता	असफलता
(i) असली	(i) ------------------
(ii) हानि	(ii) ------------------
(iii) सस्ता	(iii) ------------------
(iv) विजय	(iv) ------------------
(v) न्याय	(v) ------------------

		अ	स	फ	ल	ता	
(i)		क	ली				
(ii)						ला	
(iii)	म		गा				
(iv)					श	ज	य
(v)		न्	या	य			

7. डेविड हिन्दी भाषी नहीं है, परन्तु वह हिन्दी सीखने का प्रयत्न कर रहा है । इस कार्य में रहीम उसकी सहायता करता है । जब डेविड अशुद्ध वाक्य बोलता है, रहीम उसे शुद्ध कर के बताता है ।

जैसे:-- डेविड ने कहा, "हाथी बहुत मस्ती जानवर है ।" तब रहीम ने इसे शुद्ध किया, "हाथी बहुत मस्त जानवर है ।"

यहाँ कुछ वाक्य दिए हैं जो डेविड ने कहे थे । रहीम ने इन्हें कैसे शुद्ध किया होगा ?

डेविड के कहे वाक्य	शुद्ध वाक्य
(i) माया पानी पी रहे हैं ।	(i)
(ii) दो बच्चे खेल रहा है ।	(ii)
(iii) यह रेलगाड़ी गोरखपुर जाएगा ।	(iii)
(iv) राधा अपना सहेली से मिलने उसका घर गई ।	(iv)
(v) मोर की सबसे सुन्दर पक्षी कहा जाता है ।	(v)

8. अभय और नसीम अपने बस्ते ले कर स्कूल जा रहे हैं । देखो तो अभय के बस्ते में क्या है ?... कुछ शब्द । अब नसीम के बस्ते में झांको तो, ... अरे यहाँ तो कुछ स्त्रीलिंग शब्द हैं ।

रेखा खींच कर शब्दों को उनके सही स्त्रीलिंग से मिलाओ ।

9. नीचे दिए गए अनुच्छेद को पढ़ो और प्रश्नों के उत्तर दो ।

एक दिन स्कूल से लौटते हुए अशोक को किसी के रोने की आवाज़ सुनाई दी । यह आवाज़ झाड़ियों के पास से आ रही थी । वहाँ पहुंचने पर अशोक ने एक छोटी-सी बिल्ली को कँटीली झाड़ी में फँसा पाया । बिल्ली को निकालने में अशोक को बहुत कठिनाई हुई क्योंकि झाड़ी के नुकीले काँटे उसे बार-बार चुभ रहे थे । फिर भी, किसी तरह वह बिल्ली को छुड़ा कर अपने घर ले गया । घर जाकर उसने बिल्ली के घाव साफ किए और उसे दूध पिलाया । उस ने अपनी माँ से पूछा, "माँ, क्या हम इस बिल्ली को पाल लें? देखो कितनी सुन्दर है ।"

9.1 अशोक को कैसी आवाज सुनाई दी?

○○○

सही उत्तर पर ✓ का चिन्ह लगाओ ।

9.2 बिल्ली रो रही थी क्योंकि :

अशोक ने उसे सताया था । ☐

अशोक उसे घर ले गया था । ☐

वह कँटीली झाड़ी में फँस गई थी । ☐

उसे झाड़ी से निकाला गया था । ☐

9.3 अशोक ने बिल्ली की सहायता किस प्रकार की ?

उसे पानी पिला कर । ☐

उसे झाड़ी से निकाल कर । ☐

उसे स्कूल ले जा कर । ☐

उसे झाड़ी में छोड़ कर । ☐

9.4 अशोक ने बिल्ली की सहायता क्यों की ?

9.5 दो वाक्यों में लिखो कि आगे क्या हुआ होगा ।

10. इस वाक्य को ध्यान से पढ़ो : **"वह अपनी बहन से लम्बा है ।"**

जो चित्र इस वाक्य को दर्शाता है उस के नीचे ✓ लगाओ ।

11. **पहले क्या हुआ, फिर क्या हुआ ?** इस क्रम से दिए गए चित्रों के नीचे 1, 2, 3, 4, 5 लिखो ।

12. हम ने एक कहानी शुरु की है । अपने मन से इस कहानी को पूरा करो ।

एक दिन मंजु और संजय अपने घर से बाहर खेलते-खेलते दूर निकल गए और ...

____

____

____

____

____

बूझो
तो
जानें - 2

लेडी इर्विन कॉलेज, नई दिल्ली
Paradigms for Evaluating Primary Education

पर्यावरण अध्ययन

नाम :

आयु : लड़का/लड़की

गाँव/शहर :

स्कूल :

कक्षा :

1	5	10	14.3
2	6	11	14.4
3	7.1	12	15
4.1	7.2	13	16
4.2	8	14.1	17.1
4.3	9	14.2	17.2

दिनांक :

अवधि :

परीक्षक :

लेडी इर्विन कॉलेज, नई दिल्ली

Paradigms for Evaluating Primary Education

पर्यावरण अध्ययन

नाम :

आयु : लड़का/लड़की

गाँव/शहर :

स्कूल :

कक्षा :

1	5	10	14.3
2	6	11	14.4
3	7.1	12	15
4.1	7.2	13	16
4.2	8	14.1	17.1
4.3	9	14.2	17.2

दिनांक :

अवधि :

परीक्षक :

1. चित्र में कुछ वाहन दिखाए गए हैं। इन्हें ध्यान से देखो। इनमें से कुछ तो होंगे जो तुमने अपने गाँव/शहर में देखे होंगे। नहीं तो इनके चित्र देखे होंगे या इनके बारे में सुना होगा।

इन में से कौन से वाहन आकाश में, पानी में अथवा धरती पर चलते हैं? इनके नाम सही स्थान पर लिखो।

धरती पर　　　　पानी में　　　　आकाश में

2. नीचे लिखे वाहनों को **बढ़ती गति के क्रम से लिखो :**

रेलगाड़ी साईकिल, हवाई जहाज, रॉकिट

सबसे कम गति :

उससे अधिक गति :

और अधिक गति :

सबसे अधिक गति :

OOO

3. दी गई वस्तुएँ कौन सी ऊर्जा का प्रयोग करती हैं ? उनके सामने सही उत्तर चुन कर लिखो ।

ऊष्मीय ऊर्जा	यांत्रिक ऊर्जा
पेशीय ऊर्जा	विद्युत ऊर्जा

ऊर्जा

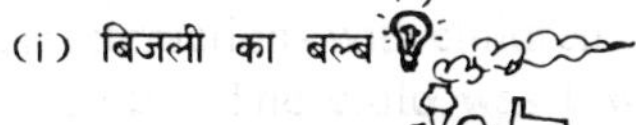

(i) बिजली का बल्ब

(ii) भाप का इन्जन

(iii) साईकिल

(iv) पवन चक्र

4.1 यहां कुछ खाद्य पदार्थों के नाम दिए गए हैं। यह पदार्थ **पौधे का** कौन-सा भाग है ?

खाद्य पदार्थ	**पौधे का भाग**
जैसे : गेहूं	बीज
आलू	
चाय	
गन्ना	
केला	
मटर	

4.2 **खाने की चीज़ों के अतिरिक्त,** पेड़-पौधों से और कौन से पदार्थ प्राप्त होते हैं ? किन्हीं पाँच पदार्थों के नाम लिखो ।

4.3 इस टोकरी में बहुत सी सब्ज़ियों के नाम हैं । इनमें से कौन सी सब्ज़ियाँ सर्दियों में मिलती हैं और कौन सी गर्मियों में मिलती हैं ?

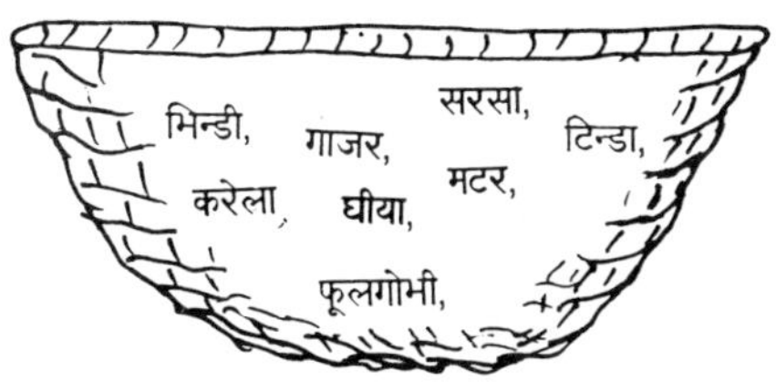

सर्दी में **गर्मी में**

5. सांस लेने में हमारे शरीर के जो अंग कार्य करते हैं उन पर घेरा लगाओ ।

हृदय	नाक	पेट	गुर्दा	श्वास-नली
फेफड़े	त्वचा	श्वसनी		

6. कई जीव अंडे देते हैं जिनमें से कुछ समय बाद बच्चे निकलते हैं । कुछ ऐसे भी जीव हैं जो पूर्णतः विकसित बच्चों को जन्म देते हैं । चित्र में दोनों प्रकार के जीव दिखाए गए हैं ।

अंडे देने वाले जीव पर [✓] लगाओ ।

○○○

तुम्हारे गाँव या शहर में सबसे अधिक बरसात किस महीने में होती है ?

अपने शहर के पास वाले गाँव का नाम लिखो ।

7.1 डाकिये को कैसे पता चलता है कि चिठ्ठी किसको पहुँचानी है ?

7.2 अगर किसी दूसरे गाँव या शहर बहुत जल्दी संदेश पहुँचाना हो तो कैसे भेजोगे ?

8. नीचे संचार के साधनों की सूची दी गई है । **रेखा खींच कर संचार साधनों को उनके प्रयोग से मिलाओ ।**

टेलीग्राम	• क्रिकेट मैच को घर बैठे देखना ।
रेडियो	• दूर बैठे किसी व्यक्ति से बातचीत करना ।
टेलीविज़न	• दूर किसी सम्बन्धी को तुरन्त सूचना देना ।
पत्र	• विविध भारती कार्यक्रम को सुनना ।
समाचार-पत्र	• त्यौहार के अवसर पर शहर से अपने भाई को लिख कर बुलाना ।
टेलीफोन	• पढ़ कर देश विदेश की घटनाओं की जानकारी प्राप्त करना ।

तुम्हारी कक्षा में कुल कितने बच्चे हैं ?

इनमें कितने लड़के हैं और कितनी लड़कियाँ ?

9. एक प्रयोग इस प्रकार किया गया : दो कटोरे लिए गए जिनमें पानी बराबर मात्रा में डाला गया । एक कटोरे को तेज धूप में रखा गया (चित्र क) । उसी समय दूसरे कटोरे को एक छायादार वृक्ष के नीचे रखा गया (चित्र ख) ।

(i) चार घंटे बाद प्रत्येक कटोरे में पानी की मात्रा कितनी होगी ? सही उत्तर के आगे ✓ लगाओ ।

चार घंटे बाद

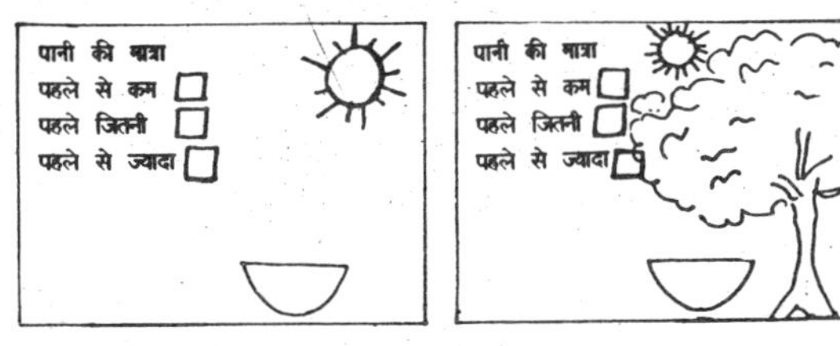

(ii) चार घंटे बाद इन कटोरों में कितना पानी रह जाएगा ? चित्र में भर कर बताओ ।

10. नीचे दिए गए वाक्यों को ध्यान से पढ़ो ।

( ) में से सबसे उचित शब्द चुनकर रिक्त स्थान भरो ।

हमारे शरीर को ऊर्जा -------------से मिलती है ।

(खाने से/व्यायाम से)

----------मिलाने से बर्फ और अधिक ठंडी हो जाती है ।

(चीनी/नमक)

पानी को गर्म करने पर------------बनती है ।

(भाप/हवा)

11. एक प्रयोग इस प्रकार किया गया - पानी के एक गिलास में बर्फ के कुछ टुकड़े डाले गए । कुछ समय बाद गिलास की बाहरी सतह पर पानी की नन्हीं-नन्हीं बूंदें दिखाई दीं । ये बूंदें कहां से आईं ? **सही उत्तर के आगे (✓) लगाओ ।**

गिलास के अन्दर से बर्फ का पानी बाहर आ गया । ( )

हवा में जो जल - वाष्प थी वह ठंडी होकर पानी बन गई । ( )

12.

					जून	1991
रवि	सोम	मंगल	बुध	बृहस्पति	शुक्र	शनि
						1
2	3	4	5	6	7	8
9	10	11	12	13	14	15
16	17	18	19	20	21	22
23	24	25	26	27	28	29
30						

कैलन्डर से महीने की तिथि की जानकारी मिलती है। यहाँ जून के महीने का कैलन्डर दिया गया है। इसको देखकर नीचे दिए गए प्रश्नों के उत्तर दो ।

(i) 1991 के जून के महीने में कितने रविवार हैं?

उत्तर [ ]

(ii) 22 जून साल का सबसे लम्बा दिन होता है। कैलन्डर देखकर बताओ कि उस दिन कौन-सा वार है।

उत्तर [वार]

13. इनमें से कौन-सा सूर्य ग्रहण है और कौन-सा चन्द्र ग्रहण ?

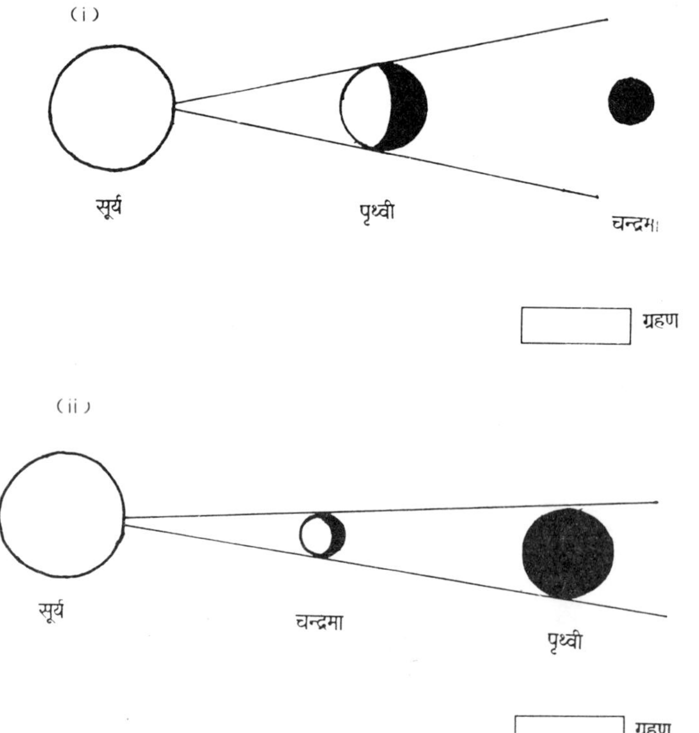

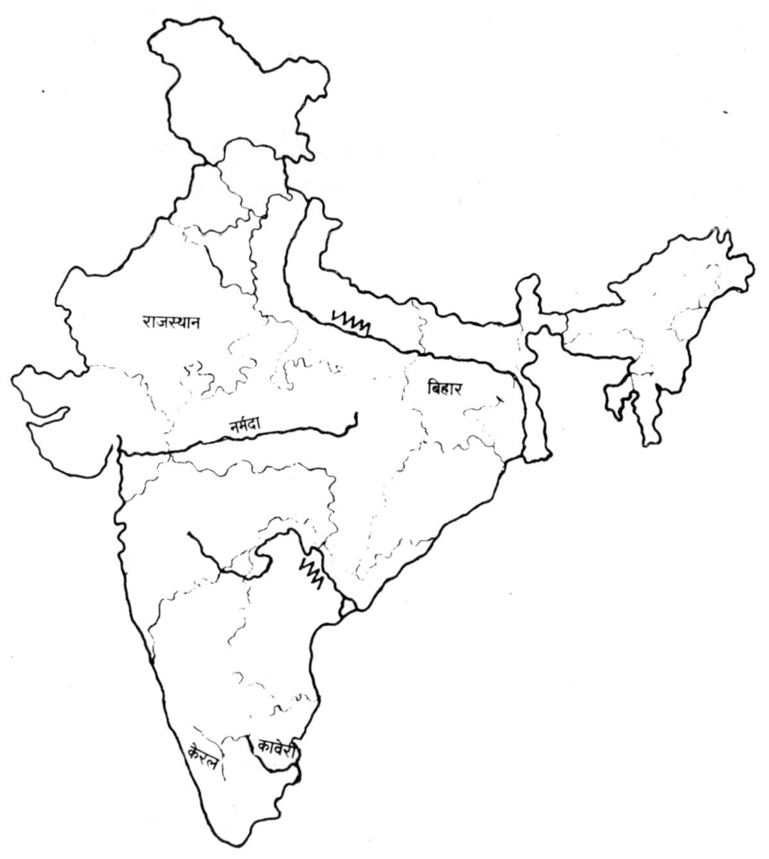
राजस्थान
बिहार
नर्मदा
केरल
कावेरी

14. **दिए गए मानचित्र को ध्यान से देखो । इस मानचित्र पर कुछ नदियों और राज्यों के नाम हैं ।**

14.1 जिन नदियों के ऊपर (ʍʍ) का चिन्ह है उनके नाम मानचित्र पर लिखो ।

○○○

14.2 मानचित्र में नर्मदा और कावेरी नदियों को दर्शाया गया है । जिन राज्यों में से ये नदियाँ बहती हैं उनमें से किसी एक का नाम लिखो।

नर्मदा --------------- से बहती है ।

कावेरी -------------- से बहती है ।

○○○

14.3 रिक्त स्थान भरो :

भारत के पश्चिमी तट पर -------------- सागर है ।

भारत के दक्षिण में ---------------- महासागर है ।

इन दोनों के नाम मानचित्र पर सही स्थान पर लिखो ।

○○○

14. भारत की राजधानी --------------- है ।

उत्तर प्रदेश की राजधानी ----------------- है ।

भारत के प्रधान मंत्री कौन हैं ?

उत्तर प्रदेश के मुख्य मंत्री कौन हैं ?

15. नीचे दिए गए पदार्थों के कोई दो उपयोग लिखो ।

लोहा :

कोयला :

16. नीचे दिखाई गई प्रत्येक बस अलग-अलग राज्य की ओर जा रही है। बसों पर लिखे शहरों के नाम देख कर बताओ कि ये किन किन राज्यों की ओर जा रही हैं।

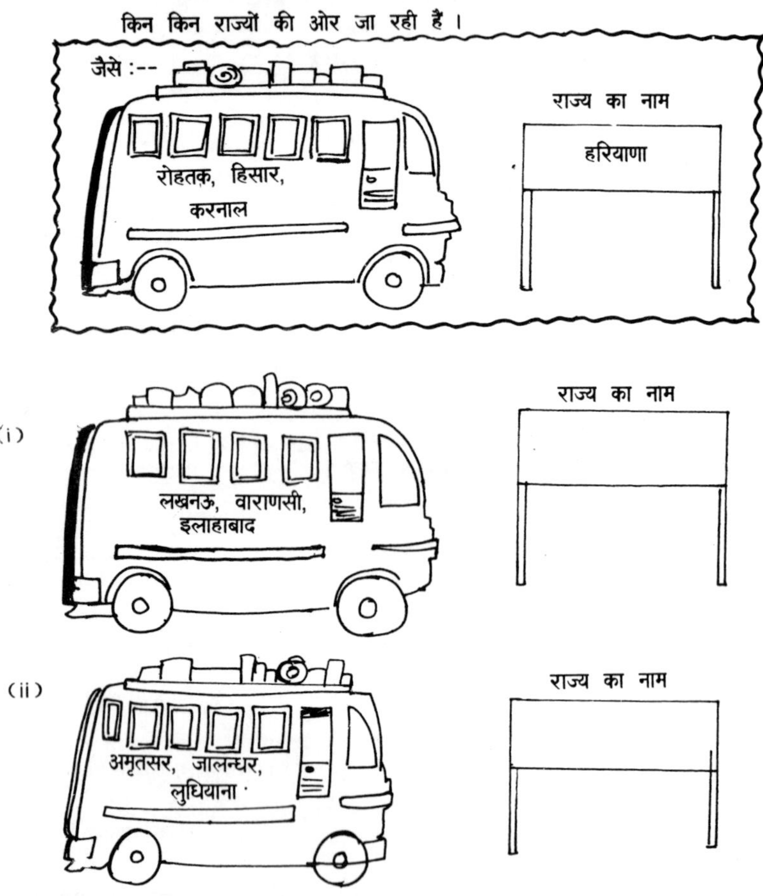

17. **यहाँ एक समाचार-पत्र में प्रकाशित समाचार का अंश दिया है । इसे पढ़ कर प्रश्नों के उत्तर दो ।**

२४ जुलाई, १९९१ नवभारत टाइम्स, नई दिल्ली ५

पहाड़ों पर पेड़ों की कटाई रोकने के लिए दिशा निर्देश

नई दिल्ली, २३ जुलाई (प्रेट्र)। केन्द्र सरकार ने समुद्र तट से एक हजार मीटर से अधिक ऊंचाई पर लगे वृक्षों की कटाई पर रोक लगाने के लिए दिशानिर्देश तैयार किए हैं।

यह कदम इसलिए उठाया गया है क्योंकि वृक्ष वायुमंडल के शुद्धिकरण में महत्वपूर्ण भूमिका अदा करते हैं। वे कार्बन डाई ऑक्साइड लेकर ऑक्सीजन छोड़ते हैं। वृक्षों की कटाई का पर्यावरण पर विपरीत प्रभाव पड़ता है।

17.1 यह समाचार किस समाचार पत्र में प्रकाशित किया गया ?

यह समाचार पत्र किस शहर से प्रकाशित किया गया ?

OOO

17.2 पेड क्यों नहीं काटने चाहिए ?

बूझो
तो
जानें-3

लेडी इर्विन कॉलेज, नई दिल्ली

Paradigms for Evaluating Primary Education

गणित

नाम :

आयु : लड़का/लड़की

गाँव/शहर :

स्कूल :

कक्षा :

1	3	7.2	11	14.2
2.1	4	8.1	12	15
2.2	5	8.2	13.1	16.1
2.3	6	9	13.2	16.2
2.4	7.1	10	14.1	17

दिनांक :

अवधि :

परीक्षक :

लेडी इर्विन कॉलेज, नई दिल्ली
Paradigms for Evaluating Primary Education

गणित

नाम :

आयु : लड़का/लड़की

गाँव/शहर :

स्कूल :

कक्षा :

1	3	7.2	11	14.2
2.1	4	8.1	12	15
2.2	5	8.2	13.1	16.1
2.3	6	9	13.2	16.2
2.4	7.1	10	14.1	17

दिनांक :

अवधि :

परीक्षक :

एक पहेली

सुनीता अपने घर से दूर निकल आई है । क्या तुम रेखा खींच कर उसे घर का रास्ता दिखा सकते हो ? देखना, तुम्हारी पेंसिल इधर-उधर न भटके !

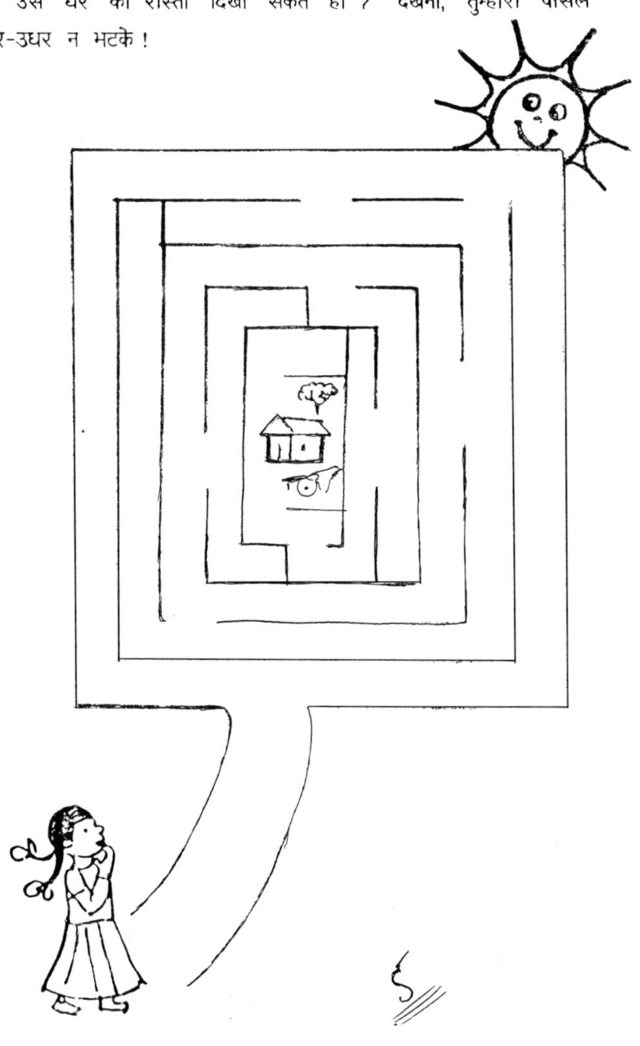

हल करो।

रफ कार्य यहाँ करें।

```
  ४२३४
+ २६९८
------

------
```

```
  ९६२४
- ४८२५
------

------
```

```
   ४६२
   ×१८
------
```

```
५ | ३६२० |
```

1. एक कैम्प लगा जिसमें चार अलग-अलग प्रांतों के बच्चे आए । चित्र देखकर रिक्त स्थान भरो ।

रफ कार्य यहाँ करें ।

हरियाणा	
बिहार	
असम	
केरल	

(i) सबसे अधिक बच्चे ------------- प्रांत से आए ।

(ii) कैम्प में कुल ----------- लड़कियाँ आईं ।

2.1 दिए गए संख्या-नाम के लिए जो संख्यांक सही है उस पर घेरा लगाओ ।

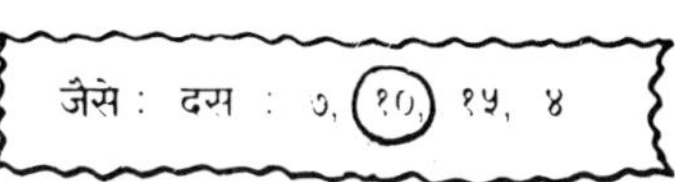

छः सौ बाईस : ६०२, ५१५, ६२२, १६२

पैंतालिस हज़ार पांच सौ इक्यावन : ४५०१, ४५५५१, ४५१, ४५०५५१

2.2 क्रम में लिखो : **रफ कार्य यहाँ करें ।**

> जैसे : १२, १५, ६, ८, २०
>
> बढ़ते क्रम में : ८, ६, १२, १५, २०
>
> घटते क्रम में : २०, १५, १२, ६, ८

अब इन संख्याओं को क्रम में लिखो :

४५०१, ४५०५५१, ४५५१, ४५१, ४००

बढ़ते क्रम में :

घटते क्रम में :

○○○

2.3 क्रम से रिक्त स्थान भरो ।

१०४७, १०४८, १०४६, --------------, १०५१

४१०५, ४२०५, ४३०५, ----------------, ४५०५

○○○

2.4 प्रत्येक संख्या में ४ का **स्थानीय मान** लिखो :

> जैसे : ४६१ में ४ का स्थानीय मान ४ [सौ] है ।

४५०१ में ४ का स्थानीय मान ४ [ ] है ।

४५०५५१ में ४ का स्थानीय मान ४ [ ] है ।

○○○

रफ कार्य यहाँ करें ।

3. उदाहरण देखकर पहेली हल करो ।

३ अंकों की सबसे छोटी संख्या [१००] है ।

५ अंकों की सबसे छोटी संख्या [ ] है ।

४ अंकों की सबसे बड़ी संख्या [ ] है ।

4. संख्याओं की तुलना करो ।

११० [>] १००, अर्थात ११० १०० से बड़ा है ।

१०० [=] ५०x२, अर्थात १०० और ५०x२ बराबर हैं ।

९० [<] १००, अर्थात ९० १०० से छोटा है।

अब नीचे केवल [ ] में > , < या = का चिन्ह लगाओ ।

९९० [ ] ९९९

२०x९ [ ] २००-२०

5. नीचे दी गई पहेलियाँ हल करो ।

रफ कार्य यहाँ करें ।

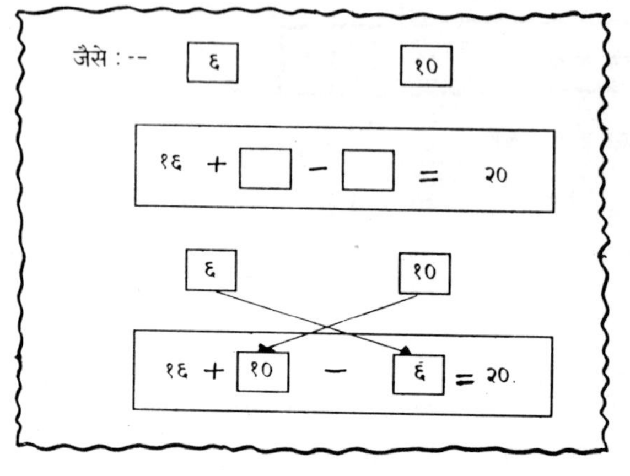

इसी तरह तुम भी □ वाले अंकों को सही स्थान में लिखो ।

(i) ५ ११

१८ + □ − □ = १२

(ii) ३ २५

□ ÷ ५ + □ = ८.

○○○

6 **जादुई वर्ग** : यह एक ऐसा वर्ग है जिसमें हरेक पंक्ति के अंकों का जोड़ बराबर होता है चाहे वह सीधी हो या तिरछी । नीचे बने जादुई वर्ग को देखो ।

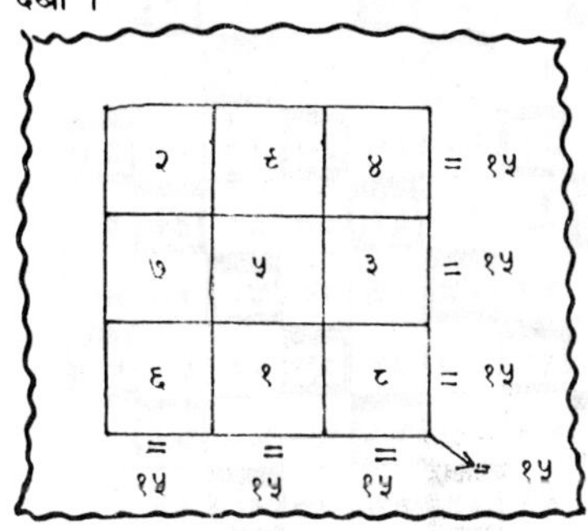

नीचे बना वर्ग अधूरा है । उसमें सही अंक भरकर जादुई वर्ग बनाओ । याद रहे हरेक पंक्ति का जोड़ बराबर हो ।

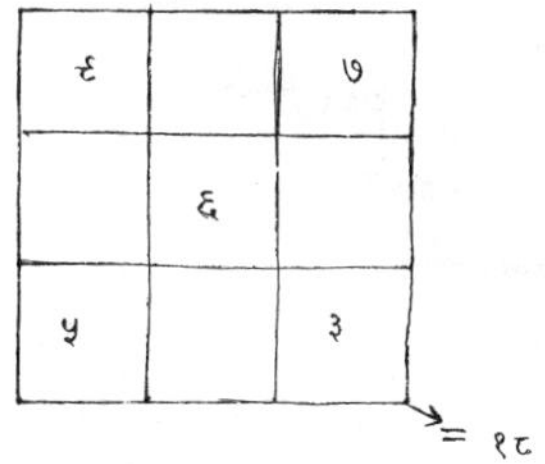

7. यह एक १०० छोटे वर्गों का बड़ा वर्ग है । इसे ध्यान से **देखो ।**

रफ कार्य यहाँ करें :

तुमने देखा होगा कि इसमें ३ के गुणज को छायांकित **किया गया है ।**

१	२	**३**	४	५	**६**	७	८	**९**	१०
११	**१२**	१३	१४	**१५**	१६	१७	**१८**	१९	२०
२१	२२	२३	**२४**	२५	२६	**२७**	२८	२९	**३०**
३१	३२	**३३**	३४	३५	**३६**	३७	३८	**३९**	४०
४१	**४२**	४३	४४	**४५**	४६	४७	**४८**	४९	५०
५१	५२	५३	**५४**	५५	५६	**५७**	५८	५९	**६०**
६१	६२	**६३**	६४	६५	**६६**	६७	६८	**६९**	७०
७१	**७२**	७३	७४	**७५**	७६	७७	**७८**	७९	८०
८१	८२	८३	**८४**	८५	८६	**८७**	८८	८९	**९०**
९१	९२	**९३**	९४	९५	**९६**	९७	९८	**९९**	१००

7.1 नीचे वने वर्ग में कुछ छोटे वर्ग छायांकित हैं । **बताओ यह किस संख्या के गुणज** हैं ?

१	२	३	४	५	६	७	८	**९**	१०
११	१२	१३	१४	१५	१६	१७	**१८**	१९	२०
२१	२२	२३	२४	२५	२६	**२७**	२८	२९	३०
३१	३२	३३	३४	३५	**३६**	३७	३८	३९	४०
४१	४२	४३	४४	**४५**	४६	४७	४८	४९	५०
५१	५२	५३	**५४**	५५	५६	५७	५८	५९	६०
६१	६२	**६३**	६४	६५	६६	६७	६८	६९	७०
७१	**७२**	७३	७४	७५	७६	७७	७८	७९	८०
८१	८२	८३	८४	८५	८६	८७	८८	८९	**९०**
९१	९२	९३	९४	९५	९६	९७	९८	**९९**	१००

उत्तर

7.2 अब नीचे बने वर्ग में ७ के गुणज पर घेरा लगाओ ।

रफ कार्य यहां करे ।

१	२	३	४	५	६	७	८	९	१०
११	१२	१३	१४	१५	१६	१७	१८	१९	२०
२१	२२	२३	२४	२५	२६	२७	२८	२९	३०
३१	३२	३३	३४	३५	३६	३७	३८	३९	४०
४१	४२	४३	४४	४५	४६	४७	४८	४९	५०
५१	५२	५३	५४	५५	५६	५७	५८	५९	६०
६१	६२	६३	६४	६५	६६	६७	६८	६९	७०
७१	७२	७३	७४	७५	७६	७७	७८	७९	८०
८१	८२	८३	८४	८५	८६	८७	८८	८९	९०
९१	९२	९३	९४	९५	९६	९७	९८	९९	१००

○○○

8.1 राजाराम ने ४२२५ रु0 में एक बैलों का जोड़ा खरीदा । उस ने ९६६ रु0 की एक साईकिल भी खरीदी । राजाराम ने कुल मिलाकर कितने रुपये खर्च किए ?

उत्तर [रु0]

○○○

8.2 शम्मी ने बाज़ार से एक किताब और एक बस्ता खरीदा । किताब का मूल्य ७ रु० ३५ पै० था । बस्ते का मूल्य किताब से २२ रु० ६० पै० अधिक था । बस्ते का मूल्य क्या था ?

रफ कार्य यहाँ करें ।

उत्तर [रु० पै०] ○○○

9. एक रेलगाड़ी २० घंटों में १२४० कि० मी० की दूरी तय करती है।

(i) एक घंटे मे यह रेलगाड़ी कितनी दूरी तय करेगी ?

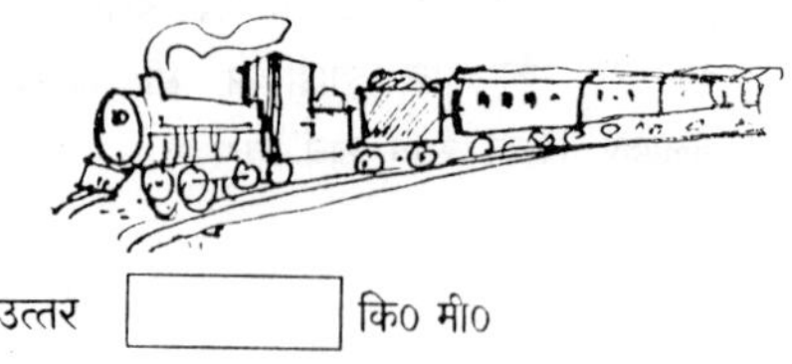

उत्तर [ ] कि० मी०

(ii) ५ घंटों में यह रेल गाड़ी कितनी दूरी तय करेगी ?

उत्तर [ ] कि० मी०

10. नीचे दिए गए चित्र को देखो । इन डिब्बों में दूध है । किस डिब्बे में अधिक दूध है ? सही उत्तर के आगे ✓ लगाओ ।

रफ कार्य यहां करें ।

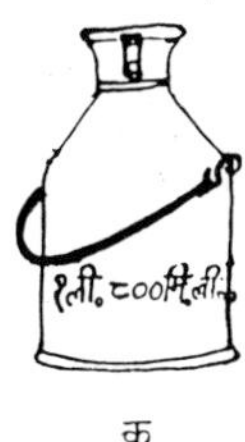

क

ख

क में अधिक दूध है ☐

ख में अधिक दूध है ☐

11. असावरी गांव शिकारपुर से ६ कि0 मी0 ५०० मी0 दूर है ।
इसका मतलब असावरी गांव शिकारपुर से--------मी0 दूर है ।

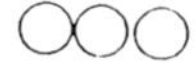

12. नीचे दिए गए चित्र को ध्यान से देखो । दोनों पलड़े बराबर करने के लिए क्या करना होगा ? सही उत्तर के आगे [✓] लगाओ । रफ कार्य यहां करें ।

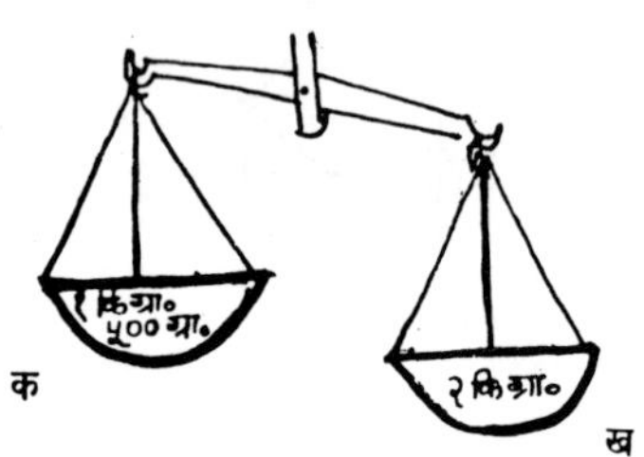

ख में ६०० ग्रा० घटा सकते हैं [ ]

क में ५०० ग्रा० बढ़ा सकते हैं [ ]

दोनों में २०० ग्रा० बढ़ा सकते हैं [ ]

○○○

13.1 घंटां और मिनट में बदलो ।

१५० मिनट = ----------- घंटे और ----------- मिनट ।

२ घंटे १५ मिनट = --------------- मिनट ।

○○○

13.2 , सन् १९६९ ई0 में मनुष्य ने चाँद पर पहला कदम रखा था । इस घटना को बीते कितने साल हो गए ?

रफ कार्य यहाँ करें ।

उत्तर [ ] साल

14.1 चित्र में घड़ी देखकर समय बताओ ।

इस घड़ी में समय है ------------

इस घड़ी में समय है ------------

14.2 एक कबड्डी मैच ७० मिनट तक खेला गया । मैच ३ बजकर १५ मिनट पर शुरु हुआ था । मैच कितने बजे समाप्त हुआ ?

रफ कार्य यहाँ करें ।

उत्तर

मैच समाप्त होने का समय नीचे दी गई घड़ी में संकेत करो ।

शुरु होने का समय

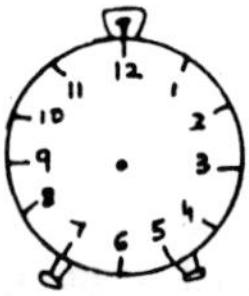

समाप्त होने का समय

15. आकृति का कितना भाग छायांकित है ?

उत्तर

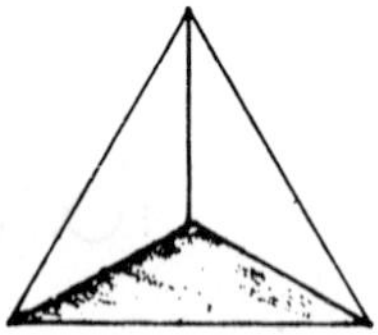

उत्तर

16.1 नीचे दिए गए भिन्नों को सरल रुप में लिखो :

रफ कार्य यहा करें ।

$\frac{९}{२७}$

$\frac{१६}{२४}$

16.2 अन्तर निकालो :

$\frac{७}{१२} - \frac{३}{१२}$

उत्तर [ ]

17. नजमा की कक्षा में ४० विद्यार्थी हैं । इनमें से ३/८ लड़कियां हैं । बताओ नजमा की कक्षा में कितने लड़के और कितनी लड़कियां हैं ?

उत्तर [ ] लड़के

[ ] लड़कियाँ

Appendix-IVa

Scoring Key for Hindi Achievement Test

Q. NO.	SCORE	RESPONSES
1.	2	or or and or or
	1	or
	0	anything else
2.	2	any 5-6 of the following responses जयपुर; रावी; लाल कलन्दर; बाँसुरी; चूहे; नदी/रावी नदी
	1	any 3-4 of the above responses.
	0	between 0-2 in the above responses.
3.1	2.	शहर में बहुत अधिक चूहे थे ।
	1	–
	0	anything else or no ✔ or more than one ✔
3.2	2	मदारी के बाँसुरी बजाने से
	1	–
	0	any other response or no ✔ or more than one ✔
3.3	2	राजा ने
	1	–
	0	any other response or no ✔ or more than one ✔
4.	2	between 0-11 errors. (spelling mistakes, omitted words & punctuation marks).
	1	12-23 errors
	0	24-25 errors

Q. NO.	SCORE	RESPONSES
5.	2	any 4-5 of the following responses.
		(i) पैसा/दौलत/सम्पत्ति/जायदाद
		(ii) हवा/पवन
		(iii) आसमान/नभ/गगन
		(iv) पहाड़/शिखर/चोटी
		(v) जमीन/भूमि/पृथ्वी
	1	any 2-3 of the above responses
	0	between 0-1 of the above responses
6.	2	any 4-5 of the following responses
		(i) नकली
		(ii) लाभ
		(iii) महंगा
		(iv) पराजय
		(v) अन्याय
	1	any 2-3 of the above responses
	0	between 0-1 of the above responses
7.	2	any 4-5 of the following responses.
		(i) माया पानी पी रही है ।
		(ii) दो बच्चे खेल रहे हैं ।
		(iii) यह रेलगाड़ी गोरखपुर जाएगी ।
		(iv) राधा अपनी सहेली से मिलने उसके घर गई ।
		(v) मोर को सबसे सुन्दर पक्षी कहा जाता है । or मोर सबसे सुन्दर पक्षी कहा जाता है ।
	1	any 2-3 of the above responses
	0	between 0-1 of the following responses
8.	2	any 4-5 of the following responses
		(i) नारी
		(ii) गाय
		(iii) लेखिका
		(iv) मोरनी
		(v) बालिका
	1	an 2-3 of the above responses
	0	between 0-1 of the following responses

Q. NO.	SCORE	RESPONSES
9.1	2	बिल्ली के रोने की आवाज़ or किसी के रोने की आवाज or रोने की आवाज
	1	बिल्ली की आवाज or meow - meow
	0	any other
9.2	2	वह कॅटीली झाड़ी में फंस गई थी ।
	1	–
	0	any other response or no ✔ or more than one ✔
9.3	2	उसे झाड़ी से निकालकर
	1	–
	0	any other response no ✔ or more than one ✔
9.4	2	कँटीली झाड़ी में फँसी थी । or दया आ गई or रो रही थी
	1	प्यारी लगी or सुन्दर लगी
	0	any thing else
9.5	2	* उसने माँ को पूछकर उसे पाल लिया होगा । * बिल्ली ने घर की सुरक्षा की । * माँ ने बिल्ली को पालने से मना कर दिया । * माँ ने कहा इसे अपनी माँ के पास छोड़ आओ ।
	1	–
	0	घाव साफ किया और बिल्ली को दूध पिलाया ।
10.	2	2nd picture ✔
	1	–
	0	any other response no ✔ or more than one ✔

Q. NO.	SCORE	RESPONSES
11.	2	(v), (i), (iii), (ii), (iv)
	1	1st 3 or last 3 in sequence.
	0	anything else.
12(i)	2	**Accuracy** – appropriate grammar (noun, verb, plurals, gender), appropriate punctuation, correct spellings.
	0	Consistently inappropriate grammar (noun, verb, plurals, gender), inappropriate punctuation, incorrect spellings.
	1	anything between the 2 response categories given above.
12(ii)	2	**Originality** – creative, non-stereotypical story, more uncommon in the group, high originality.
	1	appropriate adaptation of any other story, linking it to the stimulus given
	0	no response
12(iii)	2	**Fluency** – ease of production and sentence structure ; sequence ; flow
	0	Incoherent sentence construction sentences not linked; no sequence in content.
	1	anything between the response categories given above.
12(iv)	2	**Elaboration** – Description with appropriate length and detail
	1	Short, incomplete description.
	0	No response
13(i)	2	**Accuracy** – appropriate grammar (noun, verb, plurals, gender) and sentence construction

	0	Consistently inappropriate grammar and sentence construction
	1	anything between the two response categories given above.
13(ii)	2	**Appropriateness** – related to stimulus
	0	description completely unrelated to stimulus/no response
	1	anything between the two response categories given above
13(iii)	2	**Fluency** – Ease of production; smooth verbalization & expression of ideas;
	1	poor language production; ideas not clearly expressed
	0	incoherent speech/no response
13(iv)	2	**Elaboration** – Description with appropriate length and detail.
	1	single word naming of objects; no description
	0	No response

Appendix-IVb

Scoring Key for EVS Achievement Test

Q. NO.	SCORE	RESPONSES
1.	2	any 6-8 of the following responses धरती पर — पानी में — आकाश में * बैलगाड़ी — * पानी का जहाज — * हवाई जहाज * साईकिल — * नाव/बोट — * रॉकिट * मोटकार * रेलगाड़ी
	1	any 3-5 of the above responses
	0	between 0-2 of the above responses
2.	2	all 4 responses in the following order साईकिल, ट्रेन, हवाई-जहाज़, रॉकिट
	1	2-3 in the above order
	0	between 0-1 in the above order
3.	2.	**any 3-4 of the following responses** **(i)** विद्युत ऊर्जा **(ii)** उष्मीय ऊर्जा **(iii)** पेशीय ऊर्जा **(iv)** यांत्रिक ऊर्जा
	1	**any 2 of the above responses**
	0	**between 0-1 of the above responses**
4.1	2	any 4-5 of the following responses आलू — जड चाय — पत्ती गन्ना — तना केला — फल मटर — बीज
	1	any 2-3 of the above responses
	0	between 0-1 of the above responses

Q. NO.	SCORE	RESPONSES
4.2	2	any 4-5 correct responses e.g. rubber, gum, coal, wood, medicine, paper, oil
	1	any 2-3 of the above responses
	0	between 0-1 of the above responses
4.3	2	all 8 of the following responses **सर्दी में** — **गर्मी में** गाजर — भिण्डी सरसों — घीया फूलगोभी — टिण्डा मटर — करेला
	1	any 4-7 of the above responses
	0	between 0-3 of the above responses
5.	2	any 3-4 of the following responses नाक, श्वास-नली, फेफड़े, श्वसनी
	1	any 2 of the above or any 2-3 of the above + हृदय
	0	anything else
6.	2	all 6 of the following responses – Fish, duck, pigeon, lizard, mosquito, snake
	1	any 3-5 of the above responses
	0	between 0-2 of the above responses
7.1	2	पता/नाम और पता
	1	घर का No./ नाम
	0	anything else
7.2	2	तार/Telephone/Speed post
	1	–
	0	anything else

Q. NO.	SCORE	RESPONSES
8.	2	any 5-6 of the following responses टेलीग्राम – दूर किसी सम्बन्धी को तुरन्त सूचना देना । रेडियो – विविध भारती कार्यक्रम को सुनना । टेलिविज़न – क्रिकेट मैच को घर बैठे देखना । पत्र – त्योहार के अवसर पर शहर से अपने भाई को लिखकर बुलाना । समाचार पत्र – पढ़ कर देश विदेश की घटनाओं की जानकारी प्राप्त करना । टेलीफोन – दूर बैठे किसी व्यक्ति से बातचीत करना ।
	1	any 2-4 of the above
	0	between 0 1 of the above
9(i)	2	पहले से कम in both
	1	पहले से कम in either one
	0	anything else/no/more than one
9(ii)	2	and 
	1	either one of the above
	0	bowls shaded fully/not shaded/level same as before
10.	2	all 3 of the following responses खाने से, नमक, भाप
	1	1-2 of the above
	0	all responses incorrect
11.	2	हवा में जो जल-वाष्प थी वह ठंडी होकर पानी बन गई । (✔)
	1	–
	0	any other response both (✔) or both (✖)
12.	2	(i) 5 (ii) शनिवार
	1	either one of the above
	0	anything else.

Q. NO.	SCORE	RESPONSES
13.	2	(i) चन्द्र ग्रहण (ii) सूर्य ग्रहण
	1	either one of the above
	0	anything else
14.1	2	गंगा, गोदावरी
	1	either one of the above
	0	anything else
14.2	2	नर्मदा – गुजरात/मध्य प्रदेश कावेरी – तमिल नाडू
	1	either one of the above
	0	anything else
14.3	2	अरब सागर, हिन्द
	1	either one of the above
	0	anything else
14.4	2	दिल्ली/नई दिल्ली; लखनऊ
	1	either one of the above
	0	anything else
15.	2	4 correct uses लोहा – 2 correct uses कोयला – 2 correct uses or 3 correct uses (with a maximum of 2 in either one)
	1	total of 2 correct uses
	0	no response or only one correct use
16.	2	(i) उत्तर प्रदेश (ii) पंजाब
	1	either one of the above
	0	anything else

Q. NO.	SCORE	RESPONSES
17.1	2	नवभारत टाइम्स; नई दिल्ली
	1	either one of the above
	0	anything else
17.2	2	प्रदूषण/शुद्धिकरण/ऑक्सीजन या कॉर्बन डाइऑक्साइड
	1	बहुत चीज़ें मिलती हैं – जैसे फल, छाया, हवा
	0	anything else

Appendix-IVc

Scoring Key for Arithmetic Achievement Test

Q. NO.	SCORE	RESPONSES
1.	2	असम; 10
	1	असम or 10
	0	anything else
2.1	2	(622) and (45551)
	1	(622) or (45551)
	0	anything else
2.2	2	400, 451, 4501, 4551, 450551, and 450551, 4551, 451, 400
	1	either one of the above
	0	anything else
2.3	2	1050 and 4405
	1	1050 or 4405
	0	anything else
2.4	2	हज़ार and लाख
	1	हज़ार or लाख
	0	anything else
3.	2	10,000 and 9999
	1	10,000 or 9999
	0	anything else
4.	2	< and =
	1	< or =
	0	anything else
5.	2	(i) [5] ; [11] and (ii) [25] ; [3]
	1	either one of the above sequence
	0	anything else

Q. NO.	SCORE	RESPONSES

	2	
4		8
	10	

Q. NO.	SCORE	RESPONSES
	2	any 3 or 4 of the above
	1	any 2 of the above
	0	1 or none of the above
7.1	2	9
	1	–
	0	anything else
7.2		7, 14, 21, 28, 35, 42, 49, 56, 63, 70, 77, 84, 91, 98
	2	any 10-14 of the above
	1	any 5-9 of the above
	0	0-4 of the above
8.1	2	Rs. 5191
	1	–
	0	anything else
8.2	2	Rs. 29.95
	1	–
	0	anything else
9.1	2	(i) 62 and (ii) 310
	1	(i) 62 or (ii) 310
	0	anything else
10.	2	ख में अधिक दूध है [✓] or ✓ under picture ख
	1	–
	0	anything else

Q. NO.	SCORE	RESPONSES
11.	2	9500 metres
	1	–
	0	anything else
12.	2	क में 500 gm बढ़ा सकते हैं
	1	–
	0	anything else.
13.1	2	(i) 2 घंटे 30 मिनट and (ii) 135 मिनट
	1	either one of the above
	0	none of the above
13.2	2	22 years
	1	–
	0	anything else
14.1	2	(i) 9:15/सवा नौ/नौ बजकर 15 मिनट and (ii) 1:50/दो बजने में 10 मिनट/एक बजकर पचास मिनट
	1	either one of the above
	0	none of the above
14.2	2	4:25 and 
	1	either one of the above
	0	none of the above
15.	2	3 or 3/5 and 1 or 1/3
	1	either one of the above
	0	none of the above
16.1	2	1/3 or 2/3
	1	either one of the above
	0	none of the above

Q. NO.	SCORE	RESPONSES
16.2	2	4/12 or 1/3
	1	–
	0	anything else
17.	2	25 लड़के and 15 लड़कियां
	1	either of the above
	0	none of the above

NON-SCORING ITEMS

एक पहेली	The path traced should not cross over the lines drawn, be retraced or enter a closed path.
हल करो	6932; 4799; 8316; 724

Appendix-Va

Interview Guide to Obtain School Data

1. Name of School

2. Size of School

   i) Total number of students
   ii) Number of teachers

3. Level : Primary/Upper primary/Secondary/Sr. Secondary

4. Infrastructural facilities

   (i) Nature of Building
   (ii) Playground
   (iii) Separate classrooms
   (iv) Drinking Water
   (v) Toilet
   (vi) Electricity
   (vii) Library

5. Specific facilities for students

   i) Seating arrangement : Pupil desk/chair/bench/ mats
   Sitting space – adequate/inadequate
   ii) Ventilation
   iii) Lighting
   iv) Fan

Appendix Vb

Interview Guide to Obtain Teacher Data

I.
(1) Name
(2) Age
(3) Gender
(4) Place of birth – Rural/Urban
(5) Educational Qualification
(6) Training status
(7) Last training input
(8) Length of teaching experience
(9) Monthly salary

II.
(1) Grades taught
(2) Subjects taught
(3) Class size
(4) Average instructional work per day
(5) Number of shifts.

III. Preparation for teaching
(1) Preparation and use of monthly plan for teaching
(2) Preparation and use of daily plan for teaching
(3) Specific efforts for students lagging behind
(4) Syllabus (copy, if available)
(5) Timetable followed
(6) Textbooks followed.
(7) Frequency of homework
(8) Correction of homework
(9) Frequency of classroom assignments
(10) Frequency of written tests.

IV. Reasons for choosing teaching as a career

- Willingness to change profession.
- Perception of factors leading to job satisfaction / dissatisfaction.

Appendix-VI

TABLE 5b

Item-wise Performance in Hindi

Item No.	1	2	3.1	3.2	3.3	4	5	6	7	8	9.1	9.2	9.3	9.4	9.5	10	11	12	13
Weighted Mean	49.9	49.2	63.6	74.3	68.1	56	63.0	58.0	57.7	70.2	58.5	45.7	61.7	39.4	25.3	71.7	29.8	13.9	28
% of Chidlren performing *	72.6	67.2	63.6	74.3	68.1	71.7	80.1	73.1	69.3	78.1	68.9	45.9	61.7	44.0	29.4	71.6	34.6	40.9	94.8

* Oobtaining a score of 1 or 2 (max. score = 2)
Obtaining a score of 1-8 (max. score = 8; items 12 & 13)

TABLE 6b

Item-wise Performance in EVS

Item No.	1	2	3	4.1	4.2	4.3	5	6	7.1	7.2	8	9	10	11	12	13	14.1	14.2	14.3	14.4	15	16	17.1	17.2
Weighted Mean	71.3	60.8	12.9	31.3	13.9	58.8	30.7	60.9	46.5	33.5	35.1	33	47.7	43.3	52.6	37.8	5.3	3.6	22 5	7.1	37.5	19.6	31.9	25.4
% of children performing *	85.7	70.1	19.1	48.1	20.9	78.3	45.3	86.9	55.4	34.7	52.7	67.6	69.9	51.7	64.8	42.4	8.2	11.7	28.8	68.4	53.3	29.3	41.9	32.2

* Obtaining a score of 1 of 2 (maximum score = 2)

TABLE 7b

Item-wise Performance in Arithmetic

Item No.	1	2.1	2.2	2.3	2.4	3	4	5	6	7.1	7.2	8.1	8.2	9	10	11	12	13.1	13.2	14.1	14.2	15	16.1	16.2	17
Weighted Mean	72.6	55.5	30	37.6	50.3	20.9	39	50.2	70.6	67.6	69.8	50	35.3	34.8	63.5	22.3	60.6	29.3	37.6	37	26.5	65.3	26.2	38.5	15.4
% of children performing *	87.9	71.3	35	47.9	57.1	30.7	54.1	70.7	79.2	67.6	75.1	50.2	35.3	44.5	63.4	22.3	60.6	39.4	37.6	52.4	36.0	71.0	32.4	39.2	17.5

* Obtaining a score of 1 or 2 (max,.score=2)

Appendix-VII

List of Schools

S. No.	Name of School	No. of Students in Class V
	LUCKNOW CITY	
1.	Nirala Nagar	17
2.	Chand Ganj	3
3.	Lajpat Nagar	35
4.	Aliganj (M)	14
5.	PAC	26
6.	Aliganj (An)	19
7.	Bagh Mirza Jumma	19
8.	Chaupatia	10
9.	Triveniganj	14
10.	Napier Road	33
11.	Raj Bhawan	16
12.	Pulgama	19
13.	Bhadeva	16
14.	Billochpura	5
15.	Hasanpuria (M)	24
16.	Katra Abutarab Khan (M)	15
17.	Nishatganj (An)	8
18.	Wazirganj (An)	10
19.	Wazirganj (M)	19
20.	Mashakganj	4
21.	Tope Darwaza	15
22.	Hasanganj	7
23.	Mukaribnagar	39
24.	Mukabulganj	5
25.	Marwarigali	9
26.	Chitwapur	11
27.	Sahadatganj (K)	22
28.	Sahadatganj (B)	9
	CHINHUT	
29.	Lollai (K)	34
30.	Lollai (B)	5
31.	Chinhut - 1	56
32.	Chinhut - 2	18
33.	Malhor - 1	31
34.	Malhor - 2	16
35.	Kathauta	19
36.	Takhwa	19
37.	Bithauli	26
38.	Purabgaon	35
39.	Samadhanpur	29
40.	Matiari (B)	8
41.	Matiari (K)	12
	BAKSHI KA TALAAB	
42.	Sarrayia	35
43.	Bakshi Ka Talaab	94
44.	Itaunja - 1	71
45.	Itaunja -2	22
46.	Madiaon - 1	5
47.	Madiaon - 2	20
48.	Vijaynagar (K)	16
49.	Vijaynagar (B)	17
	AGRA CITY	
50.	Rajendranagar (B)	35
51.	Rajendranagar (K)	15

S. No.	Name of School	No. of Students in Class V
52.	Shahganj (M)	10
53.	Shahganj (An)	23
54.	Police Line	22
55.	Dubkaiya	25
56.	Malviya Nagar	11
57.	Gud Ki Mandi	38
58.	Chahshor	20
59.	Nagla Padi	16
60.	New Agra	8
61.	Ashok Nagar	21
62.	Ashok Nagar	7
63.	Moti Katra	13
64.	Moti Katra	6
65.	Bhogipura	8
66.	Tajganj	5
67.	Pak Tola	7
68.	M.P. Pura (1)	13
69.	M.P. Pura (2)	2
	BICHPURI	
70.	Midhakur	62
71.	Mohammadpur	37
72.	Barara - I	11
73.	Barara - II	39
74.	Sahara (K)	6
75.	Sahara (B)	22
76.	Patholi	31
77.	Ladamda	19
78.	Kalwari	9
79.	Sucheta	8
80.	Devretha	14
81.	Bichpuri	14
82.	Chohatna	21
83.	Sadarvan	15
	BARAOLI AHIR	
84.	Shyamo (B)	39
85.	Shyamo (K)	22
86.	Bamrauli Katara (K)	23
87.	Bamrauli Katara (B)	71
88.	Tora (B)	19
89.	Tora (K)	6
90.	Itaura	53
91.	Lakawali	32
92.	Rohta (K)	11
93.	Rohta (B)	3
	AKOLA	
94.	Balhera	20
95.	Malpura (B)	29
96.	Malpura (K)	4
97.	Akola	26
98.	Dhanoli (B)	17
99.	Dhanoli (K)	8
100.	Mankenda	40
101.	Nagla Kare	18
102.	Jarua	28
103.	Katra	23
104.	Abhaypura	29

Appendix-VIII

Difficulties in Data Collection – Tips for Researchers

Locating Schools

Locating the schools for date collection was a tedious task. The District Education Offices (DEO) provided the names of the schools and the locality but not the complete address of the schools. This meant going to the listed locality and finding out the exact location by asking people for directions. This was often very misleading. After locating a school, the team would find that the school had been shifted to another locality but had still retained its original name.

This was particularly true of urban schools. In rural areas, there were fewer schools ; most of them being government or government aided schools. Therefore, by inquiring about the 'Sarkari' school it was possible to find its location.

Posing Class IV Children as Class V Children

There were many instances of the school authorities portraying a false image of the strength of Class-V in the school.

In both Lucknow and Agra, at times the teachers would send some children of class IV to Class V. The researchers had to be vigilant. They were watchful of cues such as a child joining the group later than the others and then leaving it to join another class as soon as the test session was over ; presence of children looking too young to be class V children ; not being familiar with other children in the class etc. If this was found during or after testing, the case was dropped from the sample.

Appendix-IX

Pilot Study Report

Introduction

Education is not only a means for sustaining development but a basic human right. Tremendous progress has been made in India in the field of provision of primary education since Independence. The number of primary schools in the country has increased from 2.20 lakhs in 1950-51 to nearly 6.32 lakhs in 1989-90*. This expansion has meant an increase in the accessibility of primary school facilities and subsequently, an augmentation in enrolment.

Statistics of the number of schools and enrolment suggest moderate progress towards the goal of 'Education for All'. However, in the effort to increase the number of schools an important aspect of education, its qualitative aspect, seems to have been overlooked. Despite the high enorlment ratio, the drop-out rates as well as the rates of stagnation are high. Additionally, there is a wide variation ranging from low to high in terms of children's levels of achievement in numeracy and literacy skills, institutional infrastructure and facilities and in the teaching-learning process itself.

The National Policy on Education (1986) clearly states that the ultimate goal of primary education is not the completion of certain years of schooling, but the attainment of certain levels of learning.

Recognising the need to improve the quality and to establish standardised norms for levels of achievement, the National Council of Educational Research and Training (NCERT) has prepared a document entitled "Minimum Levels of Learning at Primary Stage", (NCERT, 1991). This document specifies the learning outcomes to be attained by the children at the end of each year during the primary school years.

The attainment of minimum levels of learning (MLL) first requires that an in-depth assessment of the existing learning levels in the primary class be ascertained. If an appreciable difference is found

* Minimum Levels of Learning at the Primary Stage, NCERT, 1991.

between the existing levels and the MLL, the teaching strategies alongwith the learning processes would require to be augmented. Evaluation of school performance thus becomes a crucial step in the process.

Significance of Evaluation

Evaluation is an integral part of the educational system. Whether done formally or informally, it involves three fundamental steps :

(i) identifying and defining the learning outcomes in behavioural terms.

(ii) constructing or selecting the tools to determine these learning levels.

(iii) using the results to improve learning.

Evaluation studies undertaken by independent researchers or institutions provide a useful entry point to the school system. Besides assessing the current learning levels of pupils, such studies provide researchers with the opportunity to re-examine the interrelatedness of teaching, learning and evaluation. Evaluation data are also useful for reporting to parents, guiding students and determining educational policies. The ultimate purposes of research and development of evaluation models should be to empower each teacher with the skills to develop her own system of assessment, which is feasible and sensitive to the needs of her group.

The Present Study

The present project aimed at developing paradigms for evaluating the academic achievement of children at the primary school level. A specific feature of this study was the emphasis on making the assessment creative, interesting for children and culturally relevant. This objective subsumed the preparation of Achievement Tests in the areas of Language (Hindi), Arithmetic and Environmental Studies (EVS) to assess the academic competencies of children who had completed Class IV (i.e. just entered Class V). The tests also had a broader purpose: to identify the lacunae in the teaching-learning process; to identify the predictors of academic performance and their relationship to school/teacher variables.

It was decided to select children who had completed Class IV (i.e. just entered Class V) for two main reasons. Firstly in most parts of the country class V is the last class in primary school. Usually in government schools, it is at the end of Class V that the child is tested for the first time. Hence, it is normal practice for teachers to work with Class V children so that they pass the examination. Conversely upto the end of Class IV, children are promoted from one class to another, without the teacher assessing whether or not the children have reached a specific level. Hence, it is more meaningful to evaluate the system that prevails over a longer period (Class I to IV) than a system that is temporarily geared up to help the children pass an examination.

Secondly, in order to assess children at the end of Class V, the data collection for the study would have to be completed in one month just prior to the school examination. It would not have been possible to locate the children in groups at any time after this. Also, it would not have been possible to assess two to three thousand children in different districts of U.P. within a month, without jeopardising the testing procedure.

The Objectives of the Pilot Study were as follows :

(1) to evolve a system of testing that is both innovative and capable of replication.

(2) to assess the levels of achievement of children in Class V in Hindi, Arithmetic and Environmental Studies.

METHOD

The primary objective of the pilot study was to establish the validity of the Achievement Tests and the feasibility of the testing procedure. These measures and processes should yield results that can confirm that the selected testing method was appropriate i.e. it provided reliable information about children's academic competencies.

Development of Achievement Tests

The major task prior to testing was the preparation of the

Achievement Tests. First, the project team reviewed literature on Indian evaluation studies at the Primary School level. Secondly, text books and syllabi prescribed for Class IV and V in Delhi and Uttar Pradesh were scrutinized. The NCERT document on Minimum Levels of Learning at Primary stage was studied for the expected competencies listed therein. At the end of these exercises, items in the areas of Language, Arithmetic and Environmental Studies (EVS) were developed. These were to serve as a pool of items from which a selection could be made.

This collection of items was given to six experts in child Development at Lady Irwin College. Based on their comments, the pool of items was revised. These items were then given for evaluation to subject teachers of Hindi, Maths and EVS and to other resource persons. The teachers were from the primary sections of two schools in Delhi generally recognised as quality schools. Their comments and suggestions were incorporated in the first draft of the Achievement Tests.

At this stage, a 3-day workshop was held for the entire project team (Chief Advisor, Faculty Coordinator and three Research Officers) to review the Achievement Tests. A few modifications were suggested and a second draft of the tests was finalised.

The test items were developed using three parameters :

(i) Development norms of children 9-10 yrs. old.
(ii) MLL prescribed for Class IV.
(iii) Content in the three subjects as found in the textbooks used in schools of Delhi and U.P.

To develop the method of administration as well as to assess children's response to the test booklets, a pre-pilot study was conducted on 25 school-going children of Class V and VI. As it was the summer vacation, the schools were closed. The children were therefore assembled and tested in the premises of Lady Irwin College. The subjects were asked to respond to tests individually or in small groups of four or five. They were allowed to take their own time and to carry over work to the next day, if they could not finish it in one sitting. This exercise was used to find out which questions children found difficult, where the instructions were not clear, which items were easy and so on. The optimal time span for administering such a test was also ascertained so that the booklet could be edited to a suitable length.

The findings of the pre-pilot study provided useful data regarding both the suitability of the items and the method of administration. The lessons thus derived formed the basis for preparing the final draft of the tests.

In addition to the Achievement Tests, an interview guide was prepared to obtain information from teachers regarding the size of school, the infrastructure and other facilities available, their training status, the nature of instructional methods used and their preparation for teaching (see Appendix 1a & b at the end of this Report).

The pilot study was conducted between early August and mid-September 1991 in Delhi and Ghaziabad (Uttar Pradesh). The sample for the study was drawn from a large cross-section of schools. Such sampling is expected to yield a wide spread of scores which will contribute to the validity of item analysis.

Sample Selection

The purposive sampling technique was used in selecting schools. The first stage in identifying the sample of students was to sort the schools into categories on the basis of the administrative body in charge (e.g. NDMC*/MCD**/Private trusts). The next stage was to select schools from each category. The criteria used to identify such schools were : Hindi should be the medium of instruction; the school should operate on a morning shift and be co-educational; and at least two schools should be in the same neighbourhood.

The Sample

In Delhi, schools run by the different local bodies, i.e. NDMC, MCD and Delhi Administration were selected. Some private schools were also selected. The sampling was done in such a way that three districts of Delhi – North, South and Central were covered.

---

* New Delhi Municipal Committee

** Municipal Corporation of Delhi

TABLE 1

Types of Schools Selected in Delhi

Type of Schools	*Number of Schools*
New Delhi Municipal Committee	3
Municipal Corporation of Delhi	3
Delhi Administration	1
Private Schools	2

In Ghaziabad (U.P, on the Delhi border), two schools run by the Basic Education Department and one private school in the vicinity of these schools were selected.

Thus, there were 12 schools in all. A total of 479 students of Class V from these schools were the subjects. The distribution of students from different schools is given in Table 2.

TABLE 2

Schools and Students Selected.

S.No.	*Type of School*	*No. of Schools*	*No. of Students*
1.	New Delhi Municipal Committee	3	116
2.	Municipal Corporation of Delhi	3	158 (62+30+66)
3.	Delhi Administration	1	49
4.	Private schools, Delhi	2	94 (47 + 47)
5.	Basic Education Deptt. Schools (Ghaziabad)	2	33 (14 + 19)
6.	Private School, Ghaziabad	1	29
	TOTAL	12	479

Data Collection

Schedule for Testing : Data collection for the pilot study was carried out from 05.08.91 to 13.09.91. Administration of the Achievement Tests (Language, Environmental Studies and Arithmetic) by a team of three Research Officers took three days in every school. An effort was made to select two schools close to one another as children were to be given only one test in a day. After the selection of two schools, work was begun in one school. On the second day, two members of the team began work in the second school, while the second test was administered in school No.1. In this way data collection for a pair of schools was completed in four days.

Administration of Achievement Tests : The testing team consisted of three members. Of these, two members administered the test in the group situation. When there were two sections of Class V in a school, each member took charge of one section. The third team member carried out the individual testing with the students and the teacher interviews. If time permitted, she also assisted the other two in administering the tests to children. The testing was carried out in a way that was child-friendly. The salient features of the testing procedure are described below :

1. The test was introduced to the children and their teachers as a 'collection of puzzles' termed 'बूझो तो जानें' (in three parts – 1, 2, 3) and not as an examination.

2. Only one test was given each day, so that fatigue would not influence children's performance.

3. On the first day, the test was begun after an introduction by the team about themselves and informal interaction with the children which included finding out their names and interests.

4. No time limit was specified to complete the test. The children were free to take as much time as they required. However, they were encouraged to stay at their desks till they completed the test.

5. When a student completed the test, he/she was asked to draw with a

crayon on the blank sheets attached in the test booklet. This was done so that the children who were still answering the test would not get disturbed. The students were asked to draw whatever they liked. If they appeared to be unable to decide, some themes were suggested.

6. At the end of the testing programme, the children were given sweets as a token of thanks.

7. There were a few children who were not present on all the three days of testing, and had attempted only one or two tests. However, their test papers were not rejected.

8. Even in a group testing situation individual attention was given to children whenever it was required. This was particularly true for some of the children who were hesitant and had to be encouraged by the researchers.

Scoring

Scoring booklets for all three subjects (Hindi, EVS and Arithmetic) were prepared describing the scoring patterns and listing all possible responses for each item.

Each test item had a three point scoring system, i.e. 0, 1 or 2. A score of 0 was given for an incorrect response, no response or an unclear response. A score of 2 was given if there was clearly the acceptable response. Partially correct responses were given a score of 1. No negative marking was done.

'No response' or unanswered items were accorded a score of zero because adequate time and opportunity had been provided to children to complete the test. In addition, each child's booklet was scrutinized to ensure that the child had not inadvertently missed out any item.

For items that had many subparts, (e.g. Q. 5 in the Hindi booklet) the total number of possible correct responses for these sub-parts was equally allocated to the three scores., In the above example, there are five sub-parts. The scoring was done as follows:

No. of Correct responses	*Score*
None or 1	0
2 or 3	1
4 or 5	2

The maximum possible score in each of the three subjects (Hindi, EVS and Arithmetic) was 50.

Data Analysis

Having obtained the children's scores, the data were analysed using a computer programme especially developed for the project. A detailed item analysis was carried out to establish the suitability of the Achievement Tests. Specifically the aim was to determine if the test items were appropriate for :

- Children in the age group 9-10 years (Class V), and
- the area of learning being assessed.

As the criterion measure for items analysis, a performance of 25 per cent or above was taken to reflect item validity. This means that when 25 per cent or more students in any school are able to successfully answer (obtain a score of 1 or 2) any given item, the item is an appropriate one.

Table 3 depicts the performance of the sample on items of Hindi, EVS and Arithmetic. A closer look at these tables indicates that while on all the items of the Hindi test more than 25% children have been able to score, the same is not true for EVS and Arithmetic items. In EVS there were two items (14.1, 14.2) in which less than 25% children were able to answer (Table 3). Similarly item numbers 11, 16.2, 17 in Arithmetic show a performance of less than 25%.

Table 4a and 4b reflect the schoolwise breakup of performance on the above items in EVS and Arithmetic. More than 25% children from both Government and Private Schools were able to obtain a

TABLE – 3

Item-wise Performance in Hindi, EVS and Arithmetic.

HINDI (n = 445)

Item No.	1	2	3.1	3.2	3.3	4	5	6	7	8	9.1	9.2	9.3	9.4	9.5	10	11	12+	13+
Percentage of children performing *	90	78	69	84	79	80	90	78	78	89	78	58	80	62	37	74	54	30	68

E.V.S (n = 459)

Item No.	1	2	3	4.1	4.2	4.3	5	6	7.1	7.2	8	9	10	11	12	13	14.1	14.2	14.3	14.4	15	16	17.1	17.2
Percentage of children performing *	94	81	31	40	29	90	61	90	64	55	79	68	90	58	66	37	10	24	33	61	43	42	40	41

ARITHMETIC (n = 447)

Item No.	1	2.1	2.2	2.3	2.4	3	4	5	6	7.1	7.2	8.1	8.2	9	10	11	12	13.1	13.2	14.1	14.2	15	16.1	16.2	17
Percentage of children performing *	88	78	45	62	61	47	78	68	70	54	70	61	30	27	64	19	43	25	33	74	28	69	29	24	6

*obtaining a score of 1 or 2 (max. score = 2)

+obtaining a score of 1 to 8 (max. score = 8)

performance of above 25% on these specific items. Although the overall performance was low, the fact that a large number of children from four schools were able to perform successfully on these items supports item appropriateness for children entering Class V.

TABLE 4a

Performance of Children According to School in EVS

Item Number	*Performance (%)*	*N.D.M.C.*			*M. C. D.*			*Delhi*	*Private Schools*			*Ghaziabad*
		1	*2*	*3*	*1*	*2*	*3*	*Admn.*	*1*	*2*	*3*	*Government*
14.1	10.5	5.0	0	0	14.5	0	16.7	0	**49.0**	6.5	0	3.6
14.2	23.5	0	0	2.3	**37.1**	22.2	21.7	16.7	**95.7**	**26.1**	0	0

TABLE 4b

Performance of Children According to School in Arithmetic

Item Number	*Performance (%)*	*N.D.M.C.*			*M.C.D.*			*Delhi*	*Private Schools*			*Ghaziabad*
		1	*2*	*3*	*1*	*2*	*3*	*Admn.*	*1*	*2*	*3*	*Government*
11	18.8	14.3	7.4	0	11.5	16.7	10.5	**26.5**	**70.2**	**37.0**	0	3.7
16.2	23.7	0	0	0	**26.2**	6.7	19.3	**26.5**	**83.0**	**50.0**	16.1	3.7
17	5.8	7.1	0	0	0	0	1.8	0	**34.0**	**13.0**	0	0

Note : Highlighted figures indicate performance above 25%

In addition to being developmentally appropriate, these items were also a part of the syllabus and the MLLs prescribed for Class IV. In other words, children are required to be proficient in these areas when they enter Class V.

In the following paragraphs are given a few examples of items found easy or difficult by children as reflected by their weighted mean scores. Weighted mean refers to the ratio between scores obtained by children, and the maximum score that can be achieved, expressed as a percentage. It is the level of children's performance on an item or set of items.

In the Hindi Achievement Test, the weighted mean for items on Grammar was 75% whereas the area on writing (dictation and guided composition) elicited a low score of 47% (Table 5).

TABLE 5

Areawise Performance in Hindi (n = 445)

Area	*Listening, Comprehension, and Memory*	*Speaking*	*Writing (Dictation and Guided Composition*	*Comprehension of ideas through reading*	*Grammar*
Item Nos.	1, 2, 3.1, 3.2, 3.3	13	4, 12	9.1, 9.2, 9.3, 9.5, 10 11	5, 6, 7, 8
Weighted Mean	71%	35%	47%	65%	75%

Areawise Performance in EVS (n = 459)

Area	*Means of Transport*	*Energy*	*Plant Life*	*Ani-mal Life*	*Means of Com-munication*	*Calen-dar*	*The Uni-Verse*	*Map Skills*	*Geog-raphy*	*Proper-ties of Matter*
Item nos.	1, 2	3	4.1, 4.2 4.3, 17.2	5, 6	7.1, 7.2, 8, 17.1	12	13	14.1, 14.2, 14.3	14.4, 16	9, 10, 11, 15
Weigh-ted Mean	80%	23%	34%	55%	51%	55%	35%	17%	47%	44%

Areawise Performance in Arithmetic (n = 447)

Area	*Number Concept*	*Addition, Subtraction, Division Multiplication*	*Daily Life Problems*	*Fractions*
Item Nos.	2.1, 2.2, 2.3, 2.4, 3, 4	5, 6, 7.1, 7.2	8.1, 8.2, 9, 10 11, 12, 13.1 13.2, 14.1, 14.2	15, 16.1 16.2, 17
Weighted Mean	52%	54%	37%	29%

In EVS the map items had a performance of only 17%. In one of the map items (14.1) two rivers of India had to be identified on the given map. In contrast the first two items in EVS (means of transport) obtained a high mean score of 80%.

Performance on 'Fractions' in the Arithmetic test was low i.e. 29%. Items requiring mathematical operations (addition, subtraction, multiplication, division) had a weighted mean score of 54%.

However, 'easy' and 'difficult' items were not eliminated from the tests but retained as they would be necessary discriminatory factors in the final test.

Test Format and Administration

The test format and administration strategies were also evaluated. On the basis of close observations of children while they were taking the tests, certain responses related to the test design could be seen. It was noticed that most children would overlook the examples used to illustrate the items. In general they would not make an effort to read the instructions or the questions preceding each item. Hence in the booklets for the final study, every example was highlighted using a box ☐ and key words in the instructions were printed in bold type. As a major region-specific modification, all the numerals in the Arithmetic booklet were changed to Hindi numerals since these were being used in the Government schools in U.P.

During the pilot test it was seen that a majority of the children found it difficult to solve some items (e.g. Multiple-choice questions, Magic square, 100 square, horizontal calculations). Although they were familiar with the concepts underlying these items, the format of the problems was novel and hence 'difficult'. Once the underlying concept of the items was explained to the group (by expanding upon the given examples) the children were able to attempt these with greater confidence.

Hence it was felt that a practice input in the new format given prior to administering the Achievement Tests could promote overall test performance of the sample.

To verify this hunch, an experiment was carried out after the completion of data collection for the pilot study. Thirty-seven children comprised the experimental group while the control group had 40 children. Both groups were students of two different sections of Class V in a Government school that was not part of the pilot study. A day before beginning testing, children in the experimental group were familiarized with the type of problems in the tests. A few examples were explained on the blackboard. During this session, the children were encouraged to participate and ask questions. After this they were given a practice sheet so that every child had the opportunity to attempt a few items, which were similar but not identical to the final test items.

On the following day the Achievement Tests were begun on both experimental and control groups simultaneously. The scores obtained by the two groups are presented in Table 6.

TABLE 6

Performance of Experimental and Control Groups in Hindi, EVS and Arithmetic

	HINDI		*EVS*		*ARITHMETIC*	
	Exp. Group n = 39	*Control Group n = 36*	*Exp. Group n = 34*	*Control Group n = 38*	*Exp. Group n = 37*	*Control Group n = 40*
MEAN SCORE	23.69	17.72	13.8	10.52	13.78	10.23
RANGE OF SCORES	7-44	3-39	1-29	1-26	2-34	0-31
S.D.	10.09	10.30	7.02	5.82	10.30	7.32
't' calc.	2.53*		2.37*		2.10*	
't' crit. = 1.667						

* difference is significant at $\alpha = 0.05$

The 't' values indicate a significant difference between the mean scores of the experimental and control groups in Hindi, EVS and Arithmetic. **In all three cases the group which received the input displayed a better performance.** A graphic display of these differences is seen in Figure 1.

On the basis of these findings it was decided to have a one-day interaction and practice, prior to testing, for all the students in the final study. This opportunity would also be used to establish rapport with the children.

Overall Performance of Children

Figure 2 displays the comparative performance of children in Hindi, EVS and Arithmetic. It is evident from this that students were performing better in Hindi, compared to both EVS and Arithmetic. The paired 't' values in Table 7 also reveal a significant difference in the scores when the three subjects are compared, the 't' values being in favour of Hindi.

TABLE 7

Paired 't' Values of Children's Performance in Hindi, EVS and Arithmetic

	HINDI	*EVS*	*ARITHMETIC*
Number of Students	445	459	447
Mean	28.53	21.40	21.82
Standard Deviation	10.85	10.71	12.13
	(Hindi-EVS)	(Hindi-Arith.)	(EVS-Arith.)
Paired 't' values	20.71*	16.93*	– 0.51
't' crit. = 2.59			

* Significant at $\alpha = 0.01$

There was, however, no significant difference between the mean scores of EVS and Arithmetic.

Fig. 1 : Performance of Experimental and Control Groups in Hindi, EVS and Arithmetic

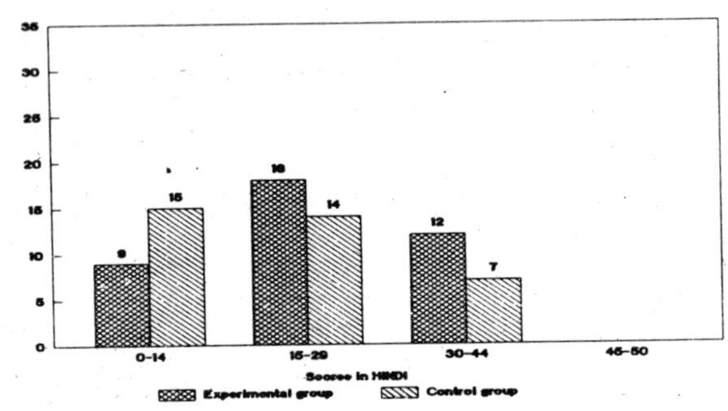

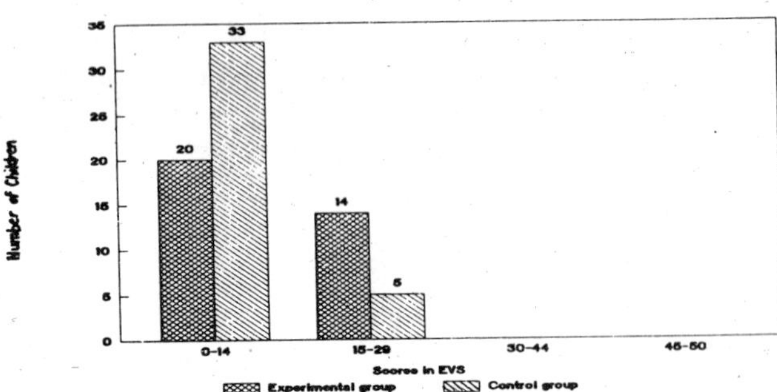

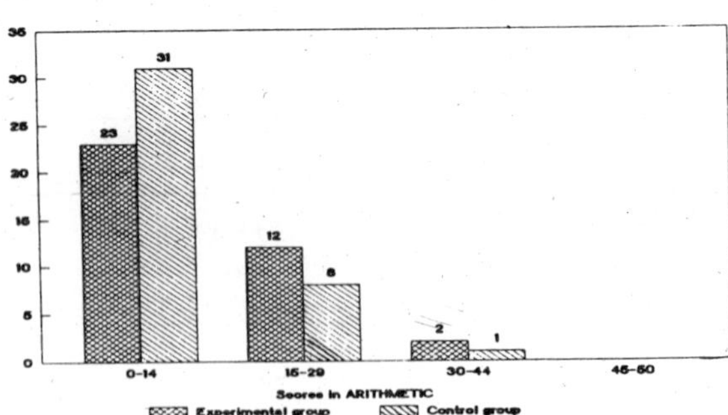

Fig.2: Performance of Children in

Hindi,EVS & Arithmetic

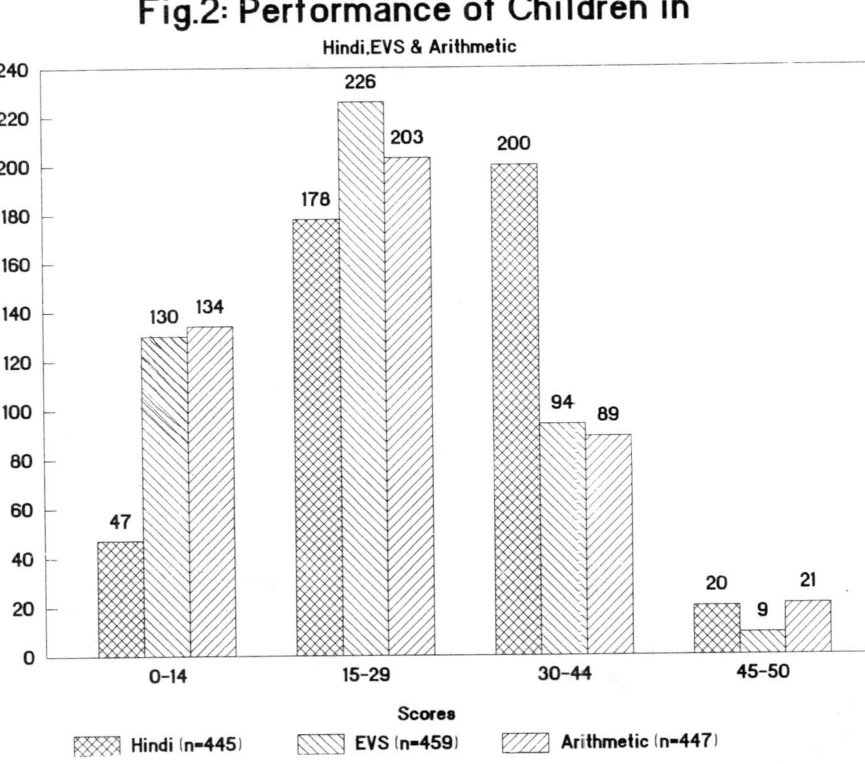

Gender Difference

Figure 3 shows the distribution of boys and girls along the range of scores obtained.

A comparison of scores across gender does not reveal any significant difference in performance on the Hindi and the EVS tests. However, in Arithmetic, the difference in scores is significant, boys having scored higher than girls.

TABLE 8

Comparison of Scores According to Gender

	HINDI		*EVS*		*ARITHMETIC*	
	Male	*Female*	*Male*	*Female*	*Male*	*Female*
No. of Students	278	167	289	170	277	170
Mean	29.07	27.93	22.02	20.51	23.09	19.63
t calc.	1.0812		1.4701		3.0014*	
t crit.	2.587		1.9655		2.589	

* significant at $\alpha = 0.01$

Age as a Variable

The children in the sample were students of Class V. They were in the age range of 7 to 15 years, with the majority being between 9 and 11 years of age.

The mean score obtained by the children in the age group 9-10 years was 29.81. Although it is considerably higher than the average score of children below this age, it was not possible to draw any inference about their performance vis-a-vis the other groups, since this group consisted of only 10 children.

Fig.3 : Performance of Children in Hindi, EVS and Arithmetic According to Gender

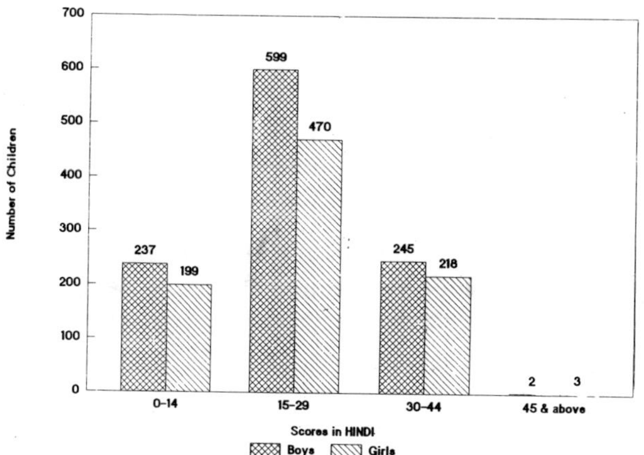

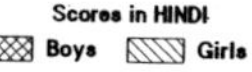

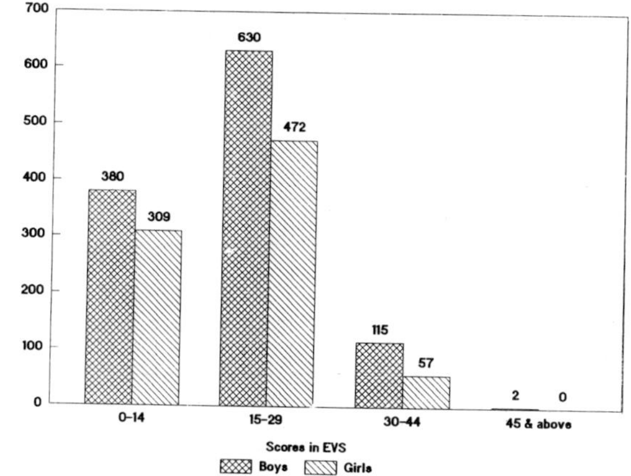

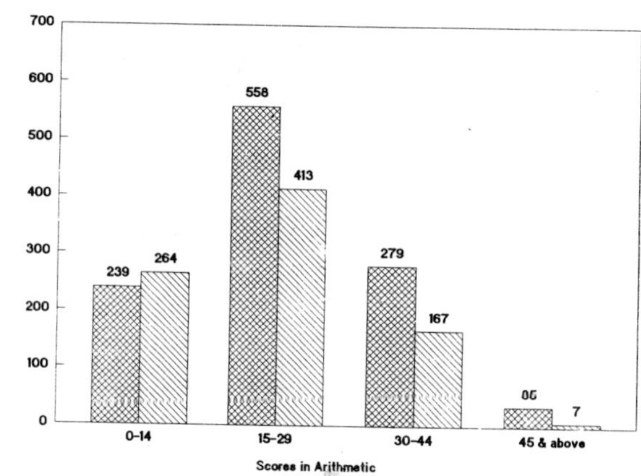

School as a Variable

Tables 9 (a, b, c,) describe the schoolwise distribution of scores for all three subjects. 't' values were obtained to compare the mean scores of all possible school pairs.

TABLE 9a

Frequency Distribution of Children's Scores in Hindi According to School

RANGE OF MARKS	*G1*	*G2*	*G3*	*Gz*	*PVT*	*Total*
0 - 4	4	-	-	-	-	4
5 - 9	13	1	-	3	-	17
10 - 14	16	5	2	3	-	26
15 - 19	23	14	1	9	1	48
20 - 24	21	29	9	6	8	73
25 - 29	11	28	5	6	7	57
30 - 34	6	39	5	3	19	72
35 - 39	5	28	10	-	18	59
40 - 44	1	10	6	-	52	69
45 - 49	1	-	1	-	18	20
50 - 54	-	-	-	-	-	-
TOTAL NO. STUDENTS	101	152	39	30	123	445
MEAN	18.85	28.48	30.35	20.00	38.10	
STANDARD DEVIATION	9.30	7.76	8.38	7.14	7.17	

TABLE 9b

Frequency Distribution of Children's Scores in EVS According to School

RANGE OF MARKS	*G1*	*G2*	*G3*	*Gz*	*PVT*	*Total*
1	2	3	4	5	6	7
0 - 4	7	1	2	3	-	13
5 - 9	18	10	3	5	2	38
10 - 14	29	25	7	10	8	79
15 - 19	29	36	9	10	16	100
20 - 24	17	33	11	4	16	81

Contd.

1	2	3	4	5	6	7
25 - 29	6	17	7	-	15	45
30 - 34	2	15	4	-	14	35
35 - 39	1	8	5	-	16	30
40 - 44	-	4	-	-	25	29
45 - 49	-	-	-	-	9	9
50 - 54	-	-	-	-	-	-
TOTAL NO. OF STUDENTS	109	149	48	32	121	459
MEAN	14.84	20.89	20.96	13.09	30.18	
STANDARD DEVIATION	7.08	8.67	9.45	5.69	10.97	

TABLE 9c

Frequency Distribution of Children's Scores in Arithmetic According to School

RANGE OF MARKS	*G1*	*G2*	*G3*	*Gz*	*PVT*	*Total*
0 - 4	18	1	1	6	-	26
5 - 9	19	9	1	10	4	43
10 - 14	22	29	4	7	3	65
15 - 19	23	33	9	8	11	84
20 - 24	19	30	4	-	16	69
25 - 29	5	30	4	-	11	50
30 - 34	5	5	8	-	14	32
35 - 39	3	5	1	-	11	20
40 - 44	-	5	2	-	30	37
45 - 49	-	1	-	-	19	20
50 - 54	-	-	-	-	1	1
TOTAL NO. OF STUDENTS	114	148	34	31	120	447
MEAN		14.46	20.58	23.03	9.74	33.00
STANDARD DEVIATION		8.92	8.56	9.61	5.36	11.50

NOTE :
G1 : NDMC Schools
G2 : M.C.D. Schools
G3 : Delhi Administration Schools
Gz : Ghaziabad Government Schools
PVT : Private Schools

These results are depicted in Table 10. A significant difference between the mean scores was shown by the school pairs marked with a tick mark in Table 10 (see Appendix II for detail at the end of this Report). This difference is consistent for all three subjects.

TABLE 10

Comparative Performance of Schools in Hindi, EVS and Arithmetic

	SCHOOL TYPE	*HINDI*	*EVS*	*ARITHMETIC*
1.	NDMC and MCD*	✔	✔	✔
2.	NDMC and DA*	✔	✔	✔
3.	NDMC* and Ghaziabad (Govt.)	✘	✘	✔
4.	NDMC and Private*	✔	✔	✔
5.	MCD and DA	✘	✘	✘
6.	MCD* and Ghaziabad (Govt.)	✔	✔	✔
7.	MCD and Private*	✔	✔	✔
8.	DA* and Ghaziabad (Govt.)	✔	✔	✔
9.	DA and Private*	✔	✔	✔
10.	Ghaziabad (Govt.) and Private*	✔	✔	✔

✔ Significant difference in performance

✘ Difference in performance not significant

* School in each pair whose performance is significantly higher.

Children of the NDMC schools performed better than those of Ghaziabad Government schools only in the Arithmetic test, there being no difference in their performance on the Hindi and EVS tests.

On the whole, the scores of students from selected private schools in Delhi were significantly higher than that of students from the government schools. This could have been predicted on the basis of earlier studies.

Among the various government schools of Delhi, the lowest mean scores were obtained by students of the NDMC schools. The MCD and Delhi Administration school children seemed to be at par and scored significantly higher than the NDMC sample on all three subjects.

Why are the children from the school systems (NDMC and MCD) performing so differently ? It would be difficult to suggest a single reason. The children in these schools came from similar socio-economic backgrounds. On the basis of teacher interviews and field visits, it was found that the family profiles of the two groups were also similar. Perhaps there is a cluster of school and teacher related factors that could account for the wide variation in test scores. These factors (given below) are only suggestive and should not be taken as conclusive evidence to explain the difference in performance between children in MCD and NDMC schools.

During the study, it appeared that children in MCD schools were more familiar with the practice of reading questions and writing their answers independently. They were more likely to read the instructions and the questions in the booklets than the NDMC school children. On talking to their teachers, it was fund that the MCD school children were given classwork and other written assignments, including class tests more regularly, compared to NDMC children. In fact, the system of class tests or assignment was not mentioned by any of the four NDMC teachers interviewed. This could be a major reason for the MCD children being more familiar with written work and the test situation on the whole.

The display boards in the NDMC schools were a sharp contrast to those in the MCD classrooms. While the NDMC classrooms were mostly 'decorated' with art and craft work and calendars, the MCD schools had charts related to what was being taught in class, depicting the organs of the human body, the food we eat, hygiene and health messages and maps of India. In fact, in some of the MCD schools, when doing the EVS test, a few children were seen going up to the map on the wall before answering a related question in the booklet. This was an indication of map reading skills being encouraged in the classroom.

In terms of school facilities, NDMC schools were better than the MCD schools. These schools had new, well constructed, spacious buildings. Toilets and drinking water facilities were provided within the school buildings. Of the schools studied, one school even had a large hall that was used for assembly and other school functions. Only one school was temporarily housed in tents, while a new building was under construction.

In comparison, the MCD schools did not have such large buildings. These schools were run in old brick barracks which were quite dark inside and poorly ventilated. Most of the classes were held in the open with the children clustered together on mats. In one of the MCD schools only Class IV and V had classrooms. Here too there were often fewer benches and desks than the number of children in the class.

Teachers of MCD and NDMC schools were from similar socio-economic backgrounds and had similar qualifications. The only difference was that the MCD teachers seemed to have a more regular system of in-service training. Four of the five MCD teachers interviewed said that they had attended workshops and science training programmes held by MCD or NCERT. Of the four NDMC teachers, only two had received any such training.

Achievement Levels

Achievement or learning upto the mastery level implies that 80 per cent or more of the children have mastered at least 80 percent of the prescribed learning levels. (MLL, NCERT, 1991). Based on this criterion, none of the school groups including the private schools attained the mastery level.

The achievement levels were on the whole highest in the Language test. Twenty per cent of the total sample obtained a score of 80 per cent or more.

The lowest achievement levels were in EVS as only 8.23 per cent of the total sample obtained a score of 80 per cent or more. In Arithmetic the performance at the 80 per cent level was by only 12.98 per cent of the students.

Private school of Delhi had the highest level of performance with nearly 73 per cent of the student achieving mastery in Hindi. The performance of children from NDMC and Ghaziabad schools was poor, since not a single student was able to get a score of 80 per cent in EVS and Arithmetic. A very low percentage of children, (1.7 and 6.9 per cent from NDMC and Ghaziabad private schools respectively) achieved mastery in Hindi (Table 11).

TABLE 11

Frequency Distribution of Children Achieving Mastery Level in Each School

SCHOOL	*TOTAL STUDENTS*	*NUMBER OF STUDENTS WITH A SCORE OF 80% OR MORE IN*		
		HINDI	*EVS*	*ARITHMETIC*
1	2	3	4	5
NDMC 1	42	-	-	-
NDMC 2	27	-	-	-
NDMC 3	47	2	-	-
MCD 1	62	5	3	3
MCD 2	30	1	-	-
MCD 3	66	4	1	3
Delhi Admin.	49	7	-	2

Contd.

1	2	3	4	5
Private 1 (Delhi)	47	44	33	36
Private 2 (Delhi)	47	24	1	14
Private 3 (Ghaziabad)	29	2	-	-
Ghaziabad Govt.	33	-	-	-
TOTAL	479	89	38	58

From the foregoing results it may be concluded that the pilot study was effective in two major aspects as follows :

(i) in establishing the validity of the test items and
(ii) in determining a reliable and child-friendly method of testing.

Hence, the content and format of the Achievement Tests were finalized for the study to be conducted in Uttar Pradesh.

References

Department of Education. (1986). **Programme of Action – National Policy on Education**, New Delhi : Department of Education. Ministry of Human Resource Development, Government of India.

National Council for Educational Research and Training. (1991). **Minimum levels of learning at the primary stage**. New Delhi : NCERT.

Appendix Ia

Interview Guide to Obtain School Data

1. Name of school

2. Size of school

   (i) Total number of students
   (ii) Number of teachers

3. Management : Govt./Pvt. Aided/Pvt. Unaided

4. Level : Primary/Upper primary/Secondary/Sr. Secondary

5. Infrastructural facilities

   (i) Nature of Building
   (ii) Playground
   (iii) Separate classrooms
   (iv) Drinking Water
   (v) Toilet
   (vi) Electricity
   (vii) Library
   (viii) School office
   (ix) Telephone

6. Specific facilities for students

   (i) Seating arrangement : pupil desk/chair/bench/mats
   Sitting space – adequate/inadequate

   (ii) Ventilation
   (iii) Lighting
   (iv) Fan

Appendix Ib

Interview Guide to Obtain Teacher Data

I.
(1) Name
(2) Age
(3) Gender
(4) Place of birth – Rural/Urban
(5) Educational Qualification
(6) Training status
(7) Last training input
(8) Length of teaching experience
(9) Monthly salary

II.
(1) Grades taught
(2) Subjects taught
(3) Class size
(4) Average instructional work per day
(5) Number of shifts

III. Preparation for teaching

(1) Preparation and use of monthly plan for teaching
(2) Preparation and use of daily plan for teaching
(3) Specific efforts for students lagging behind
(4) Syllabus (Copy, if available)
(5) Timetable followed
(6) Textbooks followed
(7) Frequency of homework
(8) Correction of homework
(9) Frequency of classroom assignments
(10) Frequency of written tests

IV. Reasons for choosing teaching as a career

- Willingness to change profession
- Perception of factors leading to job satisfaction/ dissatisfaction.

Appendix II a

't' Values Comparing Performance of Schools in Hindi

School Type	*'t' calculated*	*df*	*'t' critical at ∝ = 0.01*
NDMC and + MCD	- 9.204*	251	2.957
NDMC and + D.A.	- 7.168*	138	2.613
NDMC and Ghaziabad (Govt.)	- 0.6	129	2.615
NDMC and + Private	- 15.285*	222	2.599
MCD and D.A.	- 1.577	189	2.607
+ MCD and Ghaziabad (Govt.)	6.32*	180	2.608
MCD and + Private	- 8.90*	273	2.594
+ DA and Ghaziabad (Govt.)	5.39*	67	2.656
DA and + Private	- 4.092*	160	2.607
Ghaziabad & + Private (Govt.)	- 4.565*	151	2.352

* Difference in performance significant
+ School having higher scores

Appendix II b

't' Values Comparing Performance of Schools in EVS

School Type	*'t' calculated*	*df*	*'t' critical at* $\alpha = 0.01$
NDMC and + MCD	- 6.1081*	256	2.596
NDMC and + D.A.	- 4.5853*	155	2.35
NDMC and Ghaziabad (Govt.)	1.432	139	2.613
NDMC and + Private	-13.981*	228	2.596
MCD and D.A.	0.0671	197	2.601
+ MCD and Ghaziabad (Govt.)	6.2204*	179	2.608
MCD and + Private	- 8.165*	268	2.596
+ DA and Ghaziabad (Govt.)	4.7409*	78	2.65
DA and + Private	- 5.7951*	167	2.607
Ghaziabad & + Private (Govt.)	- 4.301*	151	2.352

* Difference in performance significant

+ School having higher scores

Appendix IIc

't' Values Comparing Performance of Schools in Arithmetic

School Type	*'t' calculated*	*df*	*'t' critical at* $\propto = 0.01$
NDMC and + MCD	- 5.5321*	260	2.596
NDMC and + D.A.	- 4.7986*	146	2.4825
+ NDMC and Ghaziabad (Govt.)	3.746*	143	2.483
NDMC and + Private	- 13.32*	232	2.598
MCD and D.A.	- 1.6120	180	2.608
+ MCD and Ghaziabad (Govt.)	9.033*	177	2.608
MCD and + Private	- 9.923*	266	2.596
+ DA and Ghaziabad (Govt.)	6.994*	63	2.653
DA and + Private	- 4.373*	152	2.35
Ghaziabad & + Private (Govt.)	- 4.469*	149	2.482

* Difference in performance significant
+ School having higher scores

Index